The Oak in the Acorn

HOWARD NEMEROV

THE Oak
IN THE
Acorn

On *Remembrance of Things Past* and on
Teaching Proust, Who Will Never Learn

Louisiana State University Press
Baton Rouge and London

Designer: Laura Roubique
Typeface: Caslon
Typesetter: Donnelley/Rocappi
Printer: Thomson-Shore, Inc.
Binder: John H. Dekker & Sons

10   9   8   7   6   5   4   3   2   1

Library of Congress Cataloging-in-Publication Data

Nemerov, Howard.
    The oak in the acorn.

    1. Proust, Marcel, 1871–1922. A la recherche du temps
perdu.   2. Proust, Marcel, 1871–1922—Study and teaching.
I. Title.
PQ2631.R63A8524   1987   843′.912   86-21087
ISBN 0-8071-1385-9

The author gratefully acknowledges permission to quote from the Chatto &
Windus: Hogarth Press edition of Marcel Proust, *Remembrance of Things Past*,
generously granted by the Proust estate, the translator, and Chatto & Windus:
The Hogarth Press, and from the C. K. Scott Moncrieff translation of Marcel
Proust, *Remembrance of Things Past*, copyright 1932 and 1960 by Random
House, Inc.

To Beverly Jarrett
dear friend
formidable editor

Contents

Preface

These lectures were given before my class in The Modern Novel at Brandeis University in the winter and spring of 1968. Their being written out in more or less full was owing in the first place to fear. Bennington College had accustomed me for nearly two decades to classes of not more than twenty pupils, often fewer than that, who could be talked with instead of at, and here at Brandeis I now was to face an audience of over a hundred; plainly a situation where works, more than grace, were to be relied on.

My notions of teaching, homemade for the most part, and received by precept and example from such colleagues as Kenneth Burke and Stanley Edgar Hyman, were (and are) simple and but two in number: 1) if you know the work to be taught pretty thoroughly, and only if you do, 2) the Lord may put the words in your mouth; though I would now add a cautionary 3), but there is no guarantee He will.

So every week during that hard and happy semester I reread Proust's book. And every weekend, like the parson of some odd faith whose sabbath falls on Tuesday, I composed my sermon, and so was able to face my century of students with nervous eagerness instead of abysmal anxiety. I was helped in composition by the circumstance that I write in just about the style I talk, and at trailing distance of the same speed; as I told this class and others over many years, if you get the knack of keeping the sentence in your head while varying its possible orders till it sounds about the way it should, you will save a great deal of paper, not to mention some vexation of spirit. I should add that this was my fourth or fifth reading of *Remembrance of Things Past*, not my first.

I first read through this immense novel not at Harvard as might have been expected, but under the less likely auspices of the Royal Canadian Air Force, at Nr. 2 Service Flying Training School in Uplands outside of Ottawa, where I was being taught to fly an aircraft oddly named the Harvard II (the reader of Proust learns to delight in connections, however trivial).

This was in the winter of 1942/1943, a severe one even for that part of the world, when the streetcars froze in their tracks and my (moderately Proustian) moustache froze white with instant age, as if for that famous last Guermantes' party, on the dawn walk down from barracks to flight line. There was little temptation, and less opportunity save for the odd weekend pass, to go into Ottawa for its metropolitan delights; and besides, one was always so tired.

The life of the cadet at Nr. 2 SFTS curiously combined military savagery (lacking only the enemy, who came later) with the coddling environment of a moderately nice nursing home. After a day of flying, waiting, ground school classes, waiting, flying, waiting, one was given supper about five, a little after dark, and in effect put to bed at six, with the freedom simply to be until lights out at nine.

Three pieces of good fortune helped me here. First, four years of college had taught me to read. Second, my beautiful boozy Aunt Ruth had given me Proust's book in English for a graduation present. And third, I was assigned an upper bunk just under one of perhaps only half a dozen ceiling lights. Had I been put in a lower bunk, I couldn't possibly have read for two or three hours a night without ruining the eyesight indispensable for flying, and my life twenty and forty years later on would have been other than it has been, and poorer.

So after a day of the military life and the life of learning to fly which made things much more bearable than the military life alone would have been, I retired most every evening to Combray, Balbec, Paris, to the continuing company of such persons as Swann, Odette, M. de Charlus, Saint-Loup, and most of all Marcel, to a whole other world built of the enchantments of language, a world which in *this* world would have been, even supposing it ever to have existed outside Proust's imagination and now mine, as inaccessible as the Grail Castle, or Kafka's. Quite apart from its power over my later life, this was a saving experience and a sacred and solitary refuge from a milieu not notable for eloquence or subtlety, a milieu linguistically so barren that one would now and then show up for Church Parade on a Sunday, just to hear a little music, a little speech not limited to (though not always other in intention than) *shit* and *fuck you.* It seemed then, and seems now, a way of redeeming the time. But it did not occur to me for a long time, for many years indeed, that there was a curious coincidence in a boy (for I wasn't much more) lying in bed reading a book about a boy lying in bed. . . .

So passed away two decades and more, and I wrote these lectures, which I put away after they were delivered, and thought little more of for the twenty more years till now. I taught a course in Proust again, at Washington University, but because I had got back to my proper and preferred class size of fifteen to twenty pupils, I had no need of formal lectures, for which I substituted my usual style of ramble and bumble.

But I am happy that owing to the kindness of the dedicatee in asking for them the lectures of long ago about long ago are now being published. It marks, for good and ill, the end of forty years at teaching, and the beginning of the forty-first. I hope my readers may have help and delight of what I have done, and be sometimes reminded of the happiness of learning.

The lectures have been left as much as possible in their original form, mostly in complete sentences though not always so, and with their warts unremoved.

Ezra Pound defined a teacher as someone "who must talk for an hour." Fine. But I add my own, in the form of a brief but characteristic conversation with a friend:

"Did I tell you my definition of a teacher?"

"No, I don't believe you did."

"A teacher is a person who never says anything once."

"O yes, I remember now, you told me that last week."

hn, 20 vi 86

A Note on References

In the text all references to Proust cite the following edition: Marcel Proust, *Remembrance of Things Past*, translated by C. K. Scott Moncrieff, and *The Past Recaptured*, translated by Frederick A. Blossom (2 vols.; New York: Random House, 1934).

Occasionally, when a point of language is at issue, an added reference is made to *A la recherche du temps perdu*, Texte établi et presenté par Pierre Clarac et André Ferré (Bibliothèque de la Pléiade, Vols. 100–102; Paris: Gallimard, 1954). Citations of the Pléiade edition are signaled with P and page numbers.

The following secondary sources have also been used and are here gratefully acknowledged:

Beckett, Samuel. *Proust*. London: Chatto & Windus, 1931.

Fowlie, Wallace. *A Reading of Marcel Proust*. Garden City, N.Y.: Anchor Books, 1964.

Hindus, Milton. *The Proustian Vision*. Carbondale: Southern Illinois University Press, 1954.

Moss, Howard. *The Magic Lantern of Marcel Proust*. New York: Macmillan, 1962.

Painter, George. *Proust: The Early Years* and *Proust: The Later Years*. Boston: Atlantic-Little Brown, 1959 and 1965.

In addition to the authors listed above, I gratefully acknowledge the assistance of Sharon Bangert, former pupil, present friend, who in preparing the fair copy for the Press improved this book in many and reckonable ways.

The Oak in the Acorn

I

1. The name of the course is The Modern Novel, and the book assigned for the term's reading might indeed be a candidate for the title The Modern Novel; its melancholy, elegance, pride, reflexiveness, all make it that. It is Proust's *A la recherche du temps perdu,* translated into English by Scott Moncrieff and Frederick Blossom.

2. Reading schedule. Perhaps the assignments will be for you unduly modest, and the pace might well be stepped up. I'd rather not, meself, as I belong to an age before speed-reading. And this is a book belonging peculiarly to solitude and meditation; indeed, I have heard that several persons who tried to speed-read their way through Proust had to be sent to asylums for more or less long periods of rest; so what you win on the swings you lose on the roundabouts.

Anyhow, I should expect the schedule to be somewhat subject to stretchings and exceptions; you observe that I forgot to leave a break in it for a midterm exam, which will come probably in mid-March.

3. On being bored by Proust. It can happen, and doubtless will. This author no less than other great men has his *longueurs* in some plenty. But to be now and then tired and impatient with his excesses, for instance of description and analysis, is one thing; to realize that this author is simply not for you, or not for you at the present moment in your lives, is quite another. The university

calendar allows you until 13 February to find this out free of charge; after that the lesson will cost you five dollars.

4. On the size of the class. Preregistration figures from last May came to 180. You will have observed that according to the terms laid down in the catalog its enrollment is limited to 15 students. The catalog, as so often happens, neglected to say who was to do the limiting, or how.

I took advice of a wise lady in the bookstore, who persuaded me that preregistration figures were based more on enthusiasm than on reality, and we ordered 100 copies, which are presently available; if more are needed they can be here by the end of next week. But I rather hope natural discouragement will work, now that we're actually in business, to keep our numbers down near 100.

5. On cutting the enrollment. I saw no way of doing this— with any show of reason—drastically enough to get the course down to 15 students with whom I might converse about the book, and about modern fiction in general; whatever I did, I should be compelled to lecture anyhow. I do not like to lecture, and most of the time do it badly; but there seems now to be no other way. And I confess to you, while feeling some helpless gratitude for your kindness in turning out in such numbers to hear me do what I do badly, that I've never cared much for the idea of being a popular teacher, especially without being a good one; it gives a man more to live up to than he can possibly do, and makes for nervousness.

Note on nervousness, and the classical Freudian interpretation of it as the speaker's own hostility projected upon his audience. Would say about this that I am not conscious of feeling this hostility toward my students, save as the unintentional occasions of my having to do a lot of work and hence a damn nuisance; but that's the way with the Freudian psychology, it's got you coming and going. If I don't *feel* the hostility, that means merely that it is as they say *latent*. One learns to live, said Merleau-Ponty, with this merciless interpretation.

6. Anyhow, the spectacle of ever so many people reading as it were in chorus this so solitary and meditative work brings embarrassing analogies to mind: telling the rosary, spinning the prayer

wheel . . . but doubtless I shall have somewhat more to say of the prayer-wheel theory of modern education later on.

7. On reading in translation. In general, a disrespectable thing to do, and quite properly condemned by the learned; however, in practice, we do it an awful lot of the time. The circle drawn on London as the center: translation snobbery is very widespread at a radius of a hundred miles and two hundred; as it ranges out, however, one rarely hears the shocked voice saying about, for example, the *Bardo Thodol*: What? you haven't read it in the original Tibetan?

Example of the Bible. It seems significant that the one exception to the rule against translations should be the one held to be universally true.

Nabokov's extended metaphor about translation in *Bend Sinister* has someone translating Shakespeare's *Hamlet*. (Paduk, by the way, was a dictator, and had, or his father had, invented a typewriter that would do one's own handwriting.)

Nature had once produced an Englishman whose domed head had been a hive of words; a man who had only to breathe on any particle of his stupendous vocabulary to have that particle live and expand and throw out tremulous tentacles until it became a complex image with a pulsing brain and correlated limbs. Three centuries later, another man, in another country, was trying to render these rhythms and metaphors in a different tongue. This process entailed a prodigious amount of labour, for the necessity of which no real reason could be given. It was as if someone, having seen a certain oak tree (further called Individual T) growing in a certain land and casting its own unique shadow on the green and brown ground, had proceeded to erect in his garden a prodigiously intricate piece of machinery which was as unlike that or any other tree as the translator's inspiration and language were unlike those of the original author, but which, by means of ingenious combinations of parts, light effects, breeze-engendering engines, would, when completed, cast a shadow exactly similar to that of Individual T—the same outline, changing in the same manner, with the same double and single spots of suns rippling in the same position, at the same hour of the day. From a practical point of view, such a waste of time and material (those headaches, those midnight triumphs that turn out to be disasters in the sober light of the morning!) was almost criminally absurd, since the greatest masterpiece of imitation presupposed a voluntary limitation of thought, in submission to another man's genius. Could this suicidal limitation and submission be compensated by the miracle of adaptive tactics, by the thousand devices of shadography, by the keen pleasure that the weaver of words and their witness experienced at every new wile in the warp, or was it, taken all in all, but an exaggerated and spiritualized replica of Paduk's writing machine?*

Or, more succinctly, Wallace Stevens: English and French constitute a single language, "Adagia."

Hindus addresses translation thus:

Since this book is to be so largely devoted to ideas and abstractions, which are nearly the same for all languages, I think that something ought to be said too about Proust's quality in French. It is to be noted as an interesting fact that his style, which seems to me the least debatable part of his equipment as an artist, has, from the very first, been more heatedly discussed, argued, and even denied altogether than any other element of his work. I have seen the view expressed that C. K. Scott Moncrieff's translation into English is so much better and more lucid than the original, that it should be translated back into French. Even if it is obvious that such an eccentric opinion merely expresses its author's taste for outrageous paradox, it still remains the statement of a view which, in a more moderate form, is apparently shared by other readers.

Proust has been described as having a style which, in its extremely intricate involvements and convolutions, is reminiscent of the obscurity attending certain German philosophers rather than of that classic purity which is the hallmark of the genius of French prose. But much as I admire Mr. Moncrieff's excellent translation, it does not seem to me to compare in quality with the original. In any writer who is a master of the music of his own tongue, the echo of that music in any other language must remain just that—an echo. Cervantes long ago accurately remarked of the relation of a literary masterpiece to its translation that it resembled that existing between the two sides of a Flemish carpet. The design on the whole is the same on both sides, but on the wrong one it is a little faded and in places gets to be stringy and disheveled.[†]

Anyhow, it's not a matter just of "knowing French"—beyond that, in a work of poetic imagining, you have the great and largely secret range of associations native to the language and drawn in by its speakers early in life, unconsciously. Here is a crude example: you might know all the words in the French original where Swann and Oriane joke about the name of Mme. de Cambremer; but the joke itself isn't in the text, you have to know it from elsewhere:

*Vladimir Nabokov, *Bend Sinister* (London, 1960), 108–109.
[†]Milton Hindus, *The Proustian Vision* (Carbondale, Ill., 1954), 20.

" . . . But surely these Cambremers have rather a startling name. It ends just in time, but it ends badly!" she said with a laugh.

"It begins no better." Swann took the point.

"Yes; that double abbreviation!"

"Some one very angry and very proper who didn't dare to finish the first word."

"But since he couldn't stop himself beginning the second, he'd have done better to finish the first and be done with it. . . . " (I, 262).

To miss the point of that, so small a thing in so vast a work, is doubtless of no moment. But it may serve to represent how many more delicate shadings we should be missing even if we could, in a school sense, translate the French.*

Still, those fluent in French should certainly read in French. Editions de la Pléiade, NRF. As to this translation, some like it and some don't. For good or ill, though, it has a distinctively recognizable style of its own—which some consider harder than the original—and it is very likely that on the final exam you will be asked to write a small parody of its tricks as a way of showing your understanding.

8. It will be a help to teacher if you compel yourselves to write

---

*Why did teacher not go on to *tell* the class this feeble joke, which he heard from his family governess at about age ten? Seems that Cambronne, a general of Napoleon's, said to an aide on going into battle, "Dîtes-moi merde, pour la bonne chance" (George D. Painter, *Proust: The Early Years* [Boston, 1959] I, 113, remembers the same joke but with a different occasion), so that ever after the better sort of French used the euphemism *le mot de Cambronne* for *merde*—ever after, or until the better sort settled down to saying "Aw, shit," like the rest of us.

Translators as a class are full of self-pity, much given to telling the rest of us about the difficulties, even the impossibilities, of their task, and to inviting our admiration for their courage and persistive constancy in meeting its huge demands. An antidote is to be found in Richard G. Stern's short story—short, but full of gists and piths—"Good Morrow, Swine," about a teacher of English instructing his French pupils that this is the appropriate equivalent of *bon jour*, with other instances to match (in *Teeth, Dying and Other Matters* [New York, 1964]). The story suggests, though it doesn't say, that translators—interpreters—probably rule the world, carrying the principle of "Good Morrow, Swine" into the UN, summit meetings, etc.

We will leave the subject of translators and translation with the thought that Proust regarded his book as a translation in the first place: "I perceived that, to describe these impressions, to write that essential book, the only true book, a great writer does not need to invent it, in the current sense of the term, since it already exists in each one of us, but merely to translate it. The duty and task of a writer are those of translator" (II, 1009).

out questions that occur to you, topics you would like to hear discussed, and present these to me either before or after class.

9. Doubtless most of the classes will deal somewhat particularly with the novel alone. But a good few, if only by way of comic relief, will be given to somewhat wider ranging discussions of the fiction of the present century in its relations and disrelations with other modes of apprehending how things are.

10. Adverting once again to the question of speed-reading. Without wanting to dictate to you what your habits of study ought to be, I should say that in my experience it is better to do a regular thirty to forty pages an evening than to try the whole assignment at once. These sentences are perhaps not unduly hard to understand, but they are often very long, so that haste more than ordinarily leads to one's getting quite lost.

11. It is scarcely necessary for me to add that I am not a scholar, and especially not a scholar in French. I can read the language, but not fast or fluently enough to read the novel in French this time. Also, while I do hope to have now and then an idea about the work on my own—which is not the same as to say an original idea—I shall very often be relying upon the scholarly and critical and artistic help afforded me by other writers, perhaps most of all by my friend and colleague Milton Hindus, and by my friend and colleague at Bennington, Wallace Fowlie.

At a faculty meeting in this room, one faction interpreted the rules to mean that a bill could not be voted upon at its first reading; another faction as stubbornly contended that a bill not voted on could not be held to have had a first reading. So it is, in a way, with the reading of Proust. Your first reading of so vast a book should properly, perhaps, go by like a dream, the dream of another life running for three months parallel with your own. It may be only at a second, later reading that you begin to make actual for yourself the instructions of this other life in their application to your own.

II

This morning I shall tell you a little about the life of Marcel Proust. Only a little, not a great deal, for there is a serious sense in which *A la recherche* is the only "life" we need or are able to deal with. Which is not at all the same thing as to say this is an autobiographical novel, but rather the opposite, that too much biography, ingested while reading the book, will produce only a blurring of the focus among three persons: Marcel the boy and young man whom we see growing, Marcel the middle-aged man who is speaking to us about him, and Marcel Proust the author, who, in projecting the two former, seems to wish to exclude himself. There are identifiable likenesses, both in detail and in theme, and of their extent and final value you shall judge yourselves; but I warn you against the historical habit of explaining either the man by the book or the book by the man; like so many things easy to do it is tempting to overdo.*

*Even the name Marcel, used on only two occasions, by Albertine (II, 429, 488; P III, 75, 157), is introduced with precautionary distancing and, so to say, the reader's connivance: "if we give the narrator the same name as the author of this book. . . ."

Not dissenting from Painter's "belief that Proust's novel cannot be fully understood without a knowledge of his life," I think nevertheless that it would have been a pedagogical disaster, and an aesthetic one, to make students on their first reading carry along such extra weight as the memory that Mme. C was really Mme. D, that Charlus was really Robert de Montesquiou, with touches of this that and the other one. Even on successive later readings, one enters into this book as into an enchanted realm where reality has no business. (But see Painter, *Proust: The Early Years*, preface.)

There are a fair number of lives of Proust available in English, and if you want to pursue the matter in detail I can recommend some of them—George Painter's two-volume study or André Maurois' *Proust: Portrait of a Genius.* For the present purpose, though, I am relying mostly on the chronology prefaced to the Pléiade edition, eked out as to detail by Wallace Fowlie's chapter "Proust the Man" in his *A Reading of Marcel Proust.* I've asked the bookstore to order several copies of this work, thinking you might find its summaries and commentaries useful in keeping the sequence of events straight—but not, please, as a substitute for the book.

1. Marcel Proust was born 10 July 1871 in a suburb of Paris; he died 1 November 1922 in Paris. At the time of his death three installments of his novel remained to be published, the proofs uncorrected by the author (six out of the sixteen volumes of the original).

2. His parents. Adrien Proust, physician and later university professor, Roman Catholic; Jeanne Weil, the mother, Jewish. Proust was baptized in the Catholic faith, and according to his housekeeper wished to be buried in that faith; in the interval, however, it is fair to say that his religion was art.

3. From infancy in delicate health. At age nine, an asthma attack, from which he appeared near suffocation. Thenceforward, a history of illnesses: coughs, colds, hayfever, asthma, insomnia. Much later one of his doctors said he had refused to cure Proust's asthma for fear of what might take its place.

4. All the same, Proust went through the usual schooling and even did a year (1889) of military service with the 76th Infantry at Orleans; according to letters cited by Painter he even, and to us unexpectedly, enjoyed it. After the year of army life he attended the Sorbonne and the Ecole des sciences politiques, found himself by temperament unsuited to the law or the diplomatic service, and began to write for periodicals. In 1896 he published *Les plaisirs et les jours* (cf. Hesiod), on which see Fowlie, p. 24. Fowlie also thinks it likely that the next three years, 1896–1899, saw the composition of *Jean Santeuil,* a prototype of *A la recherche,* which we are not dealing with in this course because it would confuse us too much; suffice it to know this work of more than a thousand pages, found

in a hat box after the master's death, was not released for publication until 1962.

5. From 1899 to 1904, studies and translates Ruskin; it is to this period and study that he owes his considerable knowledge of medieval architecture and art.

6. Death of his father, 1903; of his mother, 1905. Moves into the house on the boulevard Haussmann, 1906, where he remains till 1919, and "created the room that is the real unity of place for *A la recherche du temps perdu*" (Fowlie, 26).

7. Here in a sense the life ends and art takes over. For a period of seventeen years, from his mother's death to his own, Proust worked on his book. The first six years were given to the plan of the whole and the composition of *Swann's Way*, which he published (at his own expense, with Grasset) in 1913, after it had been turned down by several publishers, including the Nouvelle Revue Française (NRF), on the advice of André Gide. The second volume, *A l'ombre des jeunes filles en fleurs*, was published by the NRF in 1918 and won the Goncourt Prize the year after. At last he was famous, though the chronology of the novel, parallel with and yet so different from that of the life, makes it appear that one becomes famous only when fame has ceased to matter, that one is recognized by society only when the society to which one had aspired has ceased to exist.

Thus far the facts, or the mere facts—in any event but a few of them. There remain to be noted several thematic constants that affect both the life and the work, though I should beware, once again, of saying that they affect both in the same way. They are: snobbishness, illness, Jewishness, homosexuality.

SNOBBISHNESS. Proust's book is about the world, the fashionable world, and Proust himself spent much time climbing the slopes of that mountain. Letters and anecdotes and the reminiscences of others show, if the novel is not enough, that he was a snob; what the novel shows is also that he felt badly about it and outgrew the condition—unless the final incarnation, the saint and martyr of art, be thought to be the epitome of snobbery; social climbing dismissed in favor of social rocketry, after the example of Dante, whose pride

at length leaves earth and its princes far below (as at the end of
Paradiso XXII).

About this matter of snobbery. We may experience a little
difficulty in translating the terms of French social hierarchy into
our own at first, for we have neither dukes nor duchesses, neither
ancien régime nor new Napoleonic aristocracy.* We do, however,
have snobs, and may ourselves on various incitements behave indis-
tinguishably from the way in which snobs behave, and on that basis
the translation can at last be made.

Anyhow, that world of the Faubourg St.-Germain, which at
first beckoned him by its glamor and then challenged him by its
difficulty, only to appall him by its viciousness, at last became his
subject matter, or a reckonable part of it. And his depiction of the
passing of that world during the period roughly coeval with his own
life, from the Franco-Prussian War to the aftermath of the First
World War, is one of the master themes of his book, one of the
long lines on which it is planned and whose development shows the
subtlety and thoroughness of the planning, as elegant in its demonstrations of how the world happens as any proof in geometry.

We might one day take up this theme: the challenge to the
artist of a really big work, requiring years—life itself—in the
composition, of a subject matter being transformed and ultimately
destroyed by history even while he writes, where that transformation and destruction only gradually reveal themselves as his subject
matter after all.†

---

*An extended list of what we Americans lack in distinctions and institutions necessary
to composing novels was long ago drawn up by Henry James in his essay on Hawthorne:
"No sovereign, no court, no personal loyalty, no aristocracy, no church, no clergy, no army,
no diplomatic service, no country gentlemen, no palaces, no castles, nor manors, nor old
country-houses, nor parsonages, nor thatched cottages nor ivied ruins; no cathedrals, nor
abbeys, nor little Norman churches," etc., etc. It's a wonder we survived as a nation. Goethe,
to the contrary, admired the New World as a territory for imagination just because it had,
he said, "keine Basalt."

†I don't remember that we ever did. But two instances come to mind for comparison.
Thomas Mann's *The Magic Mountain*, taken up in the first place as a bit of light relief after
Death in Venice, took seven years in the telling—the same seven years that Hans Castorp
passed in his hermetic seclusion at Haus Berghof—and the Great War of 1914–1918
intervened in its composition so as to transform and expand its final chapter from novel to
epical allegory.

We do not think of Proust as a historian, though his work sometimes deals directly with the political and social developments of the period, the Dreyfus case in particular. He is a historian only as Shakespeare is in his British and Roman histories: often inaccurate as to what happened, he is supremely convincing about the nature of human happening. The comparison with Shakespeare is suggestive merely; it brings to mind also immense differences, especially in the simplicity of Shakespearian relations between individual and society, and in the dramatist's necessities for such simplicity as over against the novelist's ever more complicated web.

A related theme comes in here. If one thinks of Proust as worldly, he also provides, with remarkable art, a view of himself, or the young Marcel, as naive in the extreme—*e.g.*, his amazement at finding that people who have been pleasant and kind to his face have been saying awful things about him behind his back (Norpois, at I, 910). This in a way takes the curse off his *snobisme*, which he also displays by delegating it to other characters, such as Legrandin, in cruder and more exclusive form. The meditation on "Dromedary resting" (I, 910–11) is both funny and appealing in its combination of the narrator's brilliant analysis with Marcel's naive surprise:

> A man who is in the habit of smiling in the glass at his handsome face and stalwart figure, if you shew him their radiograph, will have, face to face with that rosary of bones, labelled as being the image of himself, the same suspicion of error as the visitor to an art gallery who, on coming to the portrait of a girl, reads in his catalogue: "Dromedary resting." Later on, this discrepancy between our portraits, according as it was our own hand that drew them or another, I was to register in the case of others than myself, living placidly in the midst of a collection of photographs which they themselves had taken while round about them grinned frightful faces, invisible to them as a rule, but plunging them in stupor if an accident were to reveal them with the warning: "This is you" (I, 911).

In similar way, T. H. White's *The Once and Future King* suffered what Conrad Aiken called "the giant footstep of interruption" from the rise of Hitler and the 1939–1945 war, and the author's attempt to cope with history involved the substitution of a second novel, *The Queen of Air and Darkness*, for the already published *The Witch in the Wood*, and a conclusion to the tetralogy, *Candle in the Wind*, in which Mordred's revolting legions are made, perhaps a little too easily, into an allegory of National Socialism. Out of all this came at last, of course, *Camelot*.

ILLNESS. Observing that Proust's life and that of the young Marcel display somewhat similar symptoms of neurasthenia, etc., we are tempted to view the novel in relation to the life. And it may be so, in some way doubtless must be so. But we cannot know the relation, not only because the novel replaces the reality of the life behind it, but also because Proust cannot be Marcel since he is the creator of Marcel and all that Marcel experiences.

Note, moreover, the advantages, if you are to portray the uncertainties of adolescence and growing up, of illness regarded as a metaphor for "normal" irritability, morbidity, sensitivity, loneliness, and introspection usually associated with this period of life. In effect, the traditional romantic association of genius with disease may be regarded as having this purely aesthetic justification—its effectiveness as drama—no matter how much it seems to come from the life of the creator.

Kenneth Burke notes about Mann and Gide that these two men, who regarded the artist variously as diseased, criminal, and perverted, did the regarding by sitting at their desks for long hours each day, working.*

JEWISHNESS. We know that Proust was Jewish on his mother's side. And by the silence of the biographies on anything to do with this circumstance beyond the mere fact we may feel entitled to draw sinister conclusions relating his snobbery with a not-very-crypto antisemitism displayed by many characters throughout the novel. Again, it may be so. But note also that whatever his feelings in the matter Proust is dealing with a society—all France, not just the aristocracy—deeply bitten by antisemitism. His major instance is the Dreyfus case, whose complicated repercussions nearly destroyed France during 1897 to 1899, or just about halfway between the German defeat of France at the time of the author's birth and the pyrrhic reversal of the war of 1914 to 1918, whose home effects

---

*We may add the testimony of Colette in her autobiography, *Earthly Paradise*, at p. 78: "The day when necessity placed a pen in my hand and I was given a little money in exchange for the pages I had written, I realized that every day of my life I would have to write, slowly, submissively, patiently, would have to match the sound to the word, would have to rise early by preference and go to bed late by necessity. The young reader does not need to know more than this about the stay-at-home, sober-minded writer hidden beneath her voluptuous fiction."

form the subject of much of his last chapters. Again, the dramatically appropriate and the autobiographical motive relate in such a way as to phase into each other. (I shall relate the course of the Dreyfus affair at the appropriate place—that is, when we come to the chapter on Mme. de Villeparisis at home, where the trial begins to reveal itself as infecting an entire society.)

Note on "country-club," or polite, antisemitism, and the Hitler kind. One is tempted to believe there was a vast difference, and that in a drastic way Hitler did us a favor by showing that the polite kind could not be excused because it led to his kind. But if you read good accounts of the Affaire Dreyfus—my sources are Barbara Tuchman in *The Proud Tower* and Hannah Arendt in *The Origins of Totalitarianism*—you are compelled to see that it simply isn't so; if the one kind is present in the salons, the other is present in the streets.*

Note too that though Proust may seem to justify antisemitism by the ridiculous and unpleasant figure of the young man Bloch, and though Bloch is at least in certain details associated with Proust himself (attendance at Zola's trial, for example, assigned to Bloch in the novel but belonging to the author in life), Bloch ultimately turns out a kindly and good man.

HOMOSEXUALITY. Whatever was known of Proust's proclivities in this matter during his life, and it must have been a great deal, it did not affect the reception of the novel until considerably later. As to Proust's being a homosexual, the matter is, according to Painter, altogether beyond doubt by now. And it is quite possible that a man named Albert le Cuziat, who served Proust during later life as "confidant and procurer," served also as the model for Jupien (Fowlie, 30). It is also possible, though less illuminating than it may at first appear, that Marcel's attachment to Albertine is the distorted reflection of Proust's attachment to a young chauffeur named Alfred Agostinelli (killed in a plane accident, by the way, while using the name Marcel Swann). All this might to an extent explain how it comes about that a young man of decent family, with his mother nearby and an old servant supervising the ménage, could

*See Barbara Tuchman, *The Proud Tower* (New York, 1966), 198, and Hannah Arendt, *The Origins of Totalitarianism*. See also *Remembrance*, I, 883.

keep his girl prisoner in the apartment for long periods of time; it might. . . . But about the poise of the novel between reality and dream, we shall find other occasions to speak. For the present it is enough to observe that no one lit upon this explanation without facts drawn from the life, and, as Fowlie observes, "the theme of perversion in the novel is of major import, but the narrator is not a pervert."

To sum up. Whatever their source in Marcel Proust's life, these four circumstances of snobbery, illness, Jewishness, homosexuality, when they become of major thematic import for the book—when they enter the imagination—do so to one effect: isolation, which is the main burden of Proust's thought. The impossibility of ever penetrating the life of another, of ever possessing entirely someone else, is heightened in its effect of suffering, is dramatized, by these further exclusions; and in a remarkable last transformation and what may rather darkly be thought of as redemption the isolation meant is that of the artist, the poet, whose loneliness is compared, in two series of analogies, on the one hand to that of the invalid, the pervert, the criminal, the Jew, the traitor, and on the other hand to that of the hero, aristocrat, doctor or surgeon, and commander of armies in the field.

III

I shall begin today's talk with a few notes of self-pity, an appeal to you for a sympathy which I hope you will remember sometimes to extend to every teacher of modern literature with whom you study.

When I went to college, modern—that is, twentieth century—literature was not much studied. We read it on our own, and delighted in secret, and fancied ourselves a cut more advanced than our teachers. Then, a few years ago, perhaps in 1960, T. S. Eliot was heard to remark somewhat wearily that he did not think modern literature should be taught in the colleges. In the interval of twenty or so years, however, modern literature had been massively studied in the colleges. I think this happened largely because a small number of works produced around the period 1914 to 1924 were very difficult, and these gave the whole of modern literature a reputation for formidable difficulty, or as it was then called "obscurity." A species of criticism grew up to meet the challenge and was presently labeled the New Criticism. This criticism concentrated its efforts on interpretation of difficult works, and its words for interpretation were characteristically technical-sounding: books were not for reading, so much as for "analysis" and "explication."*

*Considering what has happened to the language of criticism since, with its wonders of "synchrony" and "diachrony," its "différance" (so spelled in deferance to Jacques Derrida, its inventor), and its *mise en abyme* (so spelled, instead of *abime*, for no discernible

My simplified memory of the early part of this period seems to say that this kind of close reading was invented as a guide to half-a-dozen poems of Eliot, Joyce's *Ulysses*, and the songs and sonnets of Donne, plus perhaps Marvell's *The Garden*. And it was, in this country at least, a rather piratical movement, a little outside the academy, and rather given to sniping at historical scholarship and the Ph.D. for being critically inadequate and for directing attention away from the work being discussed rather than to it. To be as brief as possible about it (and I warn you that this is only my opinion, or dream, about what happened): the original freebooters received the Dean's pardon and presently become full professors. The movement, by now named New Criticism for good or ill, invaded the academy, where it flourished wondrous well and sent out invading armies of bright young instructors in the direction of Shakespeare's plays and the modern novel even while as a method this sort of criticism was subjugating such outlying countries as psychoanalysis, anthropology, and theology; and for quite a while, maybe fifteen years dating from 1940, all this looked extremely good. Students read so atrociously, perhaps, that it was no trick at all to teach them to read better, for the only direction open to them was up, as I. A. Richards had shown in his *Practical Criticism* a long while before. And the teaching of modern literature was massively instated in college education. Whereupon two other things happened. At least two. The teaching had some effect, maybe only by osmosis or as contaminating the atmosphere so that everyone breathed it in willy nilly, so that the teacher could no longer astound his pupils by pointing out, say, the ambiguity (as it was called) in the word *die* when used by an Elizabethan poet. For the pupils knew that already. The other thing that had happened, though, was that for the most part modern writers were letting us down. Either they were difficult in a way that was not amenable to New-Critical treatment (Pound in the *Cantos*), or they just weren't very difficult.

---

reason, unless it is Old French), the language of the then New Criticism (so named by John Crowe Ransom in his 1940 book of that title) now looks delightfully homey and even a touch naive.

But by now a great deal of time and money and learning and feeling had been invested in the industry, and no one could easily quit. To this predicament there were in the main, again, two solutions that blended readily into one: teach easy works as though they were hard ones; and make criticism itself much harder, more systematic, more rigorous, more of a *method*. This answered tolerably for a while, but one could not get rid of an uneasy sense that it was leading in the direction of idolatry. Moreover, a great many people, especially students, began to be sick of the whole damn business, and I should judge that from the rise of the Beat movement in the middle 1950s there began a corresponding decline in the fortunes of whatever was represented by the New Criticism; at best, the habit of patient and minute scrutiny of a literary work in and for itself, coupled with a search for its remotest relations in other fields of study. Thus I suspect—chiefly from my poetry-writing pupils—that people went back to reading as casually and sloppily as ever, and it was as if the New Criticism had never done its work. This is of course the lament of a middle-aged teacher, and it's common, you will understand, for the middle-aged to project their own declining powers upon the world at large and upon their students in especial. Allowing that, as Saint Augustine says, these things are true in a way because they are false in a way, I shall make some application of the foregoing to the difficulties I anticipate in the teaching of Proust's novel.

Remembrance of Things Past is I think a difficult work, but rather for the spirit and the feelings and the senses than for the critical intelligence. For that last faculty, it is not difficult, because Proust explains it himself at such very great length throughout. Whereupon I warn myself that it would be a teacherly disaster for me to spend much time reading great swatches of the text to you in order to say afterward rather badly what the author has said so well concerning what they mean. On the other hand, it would be equally catastrophic for me to read you passages only in order to exclaim "How beautiful!" While we have a highly developed terminology for dealing with what things mean, we have little or none for dealing with how things feel; with an author's way of sensing, his way of putting the world together by, as it were, his own individual variation of the transcendental *a priori* unity of apperception, or with the soul, rather than the meaning, of his work. And it is with these things that I hope to be chiefly concerned.

I just wanted your sympathy.

About the opening of Proust's novel, and some thoughts on the method of its composition.

What I have to say is very simple. But saying the simplest and most obvious things is, I find, the best way to get a work of the imagination to open itself to you and tell you something more than the mere words on the page. That is because a book is more like a mind than it is like a thought; it is no doubt a much simplified model for the mind, yet it may be the best model we are able to find.

The first things this book tells us about are sleeping and waking and the passage of time. Whoever is speaking to us in the first person has as yet no identity, scarcely a personality or a "character" in the common novelistic acceptation of that doubtful word. He is a voice at night. What night? We do not know, though we soon come to understand (I, 6) that he is a grown-up returned to visit the places where he grew up—*suivre au claire de lune ces chemins où je jouais jadis au soleil,* he says. He is a kind of revenant, and there is to begin with something a trifle ghostly about the dislocation of his talk, its hovering in the night as though not definitely fixed in time.

The title of Proust's book says it is about time, lost time, time past, and trying to find it—a strange project, for everyone knows that when time passes it is gone beyond recovery. But the word *recherche* is an odd one, for it may mean not only search but research, not only quest but investigation and inquiry.

The manner of composition in this "Overture"* is *musical.* I shall return to this subject and try to show that it has here more than the usual complimentary cant sense. For now I shall but say that Proust does not open in a conventional storytelling way by giving us information obviously useful, such as "Once upon a time

*This is the translator's invention—I think an apt one. The first chapter of the original is untitled.

there was a certain man who had three sons," an opening hallowed by fairy tale and still echoing recognizably in *The Brothers Karamazov*. Proust seems instead to begin at random, though we observe that the word *time* is at the very beginning, just as it is at the very end. And he skips about from one thing to another, on no immediately obvious principle of continuity. Which introduces still another theme, one related to time, in addition to sleeping and waking: memory. For your relation to time in memory is not at all like your relation to time in living: all that you are able to remember is in a sense equidistant from you and equally accessible; somewhat as it is in dreams, save that with memory it is more at the command of the will. By no means altogether, but more.

As well as being musical, the manner of composition may be called Impressionist, after the example of the Impressionist painters who work by applying to their canvas as it were the minute atomic structure of light and appearance to make forms that can be understood in their gross, literal, worldly sense only at a certain distance. So too with this narrator, who mentions people and places without explanation: we shall have to achieve a certain distance in order to begin to understand, for example, who Gilberte is, and what places were Combray, Balbec, Doncières, and the rest.

Now this principle drawn from the Impressionist painters enters literature perhaps with Flaubert and with James, with their concern for "rendering" and the means of representation. It is explicitly present, and described, in Ford Madox Ford's *Joseph Conrad: A Personal Reminiscence*, where Ford asserts the principle thus: Life does not narrate. It makes impressions on our minds. This subject is one I hope to take up by its interesting self at another lecture; right now I want to stick to my thematic exposition.

Another very simple thing, maybe the simplest. The book's beginning enunciates two themes, the inside and the outside. There is on one side the mind, describing, analyzing, remembering, evaluating; on the other, the world, society, a life now mostly lived and in the past. How are these two to be put together?

I answer: in a very simple way. This novel is the story of a man's search for his vocation, a vocation, he hopes, in art, in literature; but the object of the search is, after all, the self, and the book's object is, again, itself; its own composition is the answer to the one question we all ask: What shall I do with my life? which is in its own terms the same question as What must I do to be saved? For the vocation of the artist, in this novel, is seriously taken to be sacred, and its achievement tantamount in its own terms to salvation in the terms of religion. As Milton Hindus has said, it is as though Dante had undertaken to write the *Comedy* without Christianity, and that is a comparison I find illuminating.

For Dante's poem, like this one, is about sleep and waking. It begins by saying that in the middle of his life the poet "found himself again"—*mi ritrovai*—and a few lines later makes clear that the dark wood in which he did so is indeed the sleep of this earthly existence:

> I' non so ben ridir com'io v'entrai;
> Tant' era pien di sonno in su quel punto,
> Che la verace via abandonnai.*

For Proust, this sleeping and this dark wood may be thought of as habit, or custom, that "amenageuse habile mais bien lente," and society, or the world, respectively. And I think we shall be rightly led if we pay attention to what Dante says about his book, in dedicating the last part of it to Can Grande della Scala:

> sciendum est quod istius operis non est simplex sensus, immo dici potest *polysemos,* hoc est plurimum sensuum; nam primus sensus est qui habetur per literam, alius est qui habetur per significata per literam. Et primus dicitur literalis, secundus vero allegoricus, sive moralis, sive anagogicus. Qui modus tractandi, ut melius pateat, potest considerari in his versibus: "In exitu Israel de Aegypto, domus Iacob de populo barbero, facta est Iudaea sanctificatio eius, Israel potestas eius." Nam si ad literam solam inspiciamus, significatur novis exitus filiorum Israel de Aegypto, tempore Moysi; si ad allegoriam, nobis significatur nostra redemptio facta per Christum; si ad moralem sensum, significatur nobis conversio animae de loctu et miseria peccati ad statum gratiae; si ad anagogicum, significatur existus animae sanctae ab huius corruptionis servitute ad aeternae gloriae libertatem.†

---

*"I can't well tell you how I came there [the Dark Wood of Inferno I–II],/so full of sleep was I at the moment/ that I left the true way."

† The introduction of this bit of Latin, from Dante's Tenth Letter dedicating (and sort of explaining) the *Paradiso* to his patron Can Grande de la Scala, shows Teacher laboring mightily to impress the class; the English is roughly as follows:

Jerusalem is literally a city of Palestine, allegorically the Church, morally the believing soul, anagogically the heavenly Jerusalem.

Note about this that the anagoge is the universal and reflexive sense, having to do with the end of time and the resurrection of the body, that most difficult of beliefs; it relates to what I said a few moments ago about the object of the search being the self and the object of the book being the book itself.

We shall be helped, I believe, if we remember through the complexities of *A la recherche du temps perdu* that it is quite simply about how shall a man live; and the "world," for Proust, whether in Combray or the Faubourg, is what it has always been, and what it was for Dante, for Bunyan, for Goethe, and for others who have told this first and last of stories—a dark place having but the one advantage that in total darkness the only thing possible to be seen if offered will be a light.

Perhaps the idea of art as capable of salvation, of art as a religion, is not so much with us. One has the impression, anyhow, that literary art these days is used for other purposes: social criticism, protest, self-indulgence, self-expression, and realism (which,

---

It should be known that this work is not of simple sense, but rather may be called *polysemous*, that is, of several senses; for the first sense is what you get from the letter, and the others are what you get from what the letter signifies. The first is called the literal, and the others are the allegorical, or the moral, or the anagogical. For your better understanding, this way of doing things may be exemplified by the following verses: "When Israel came up out of Egypt, and the house of Jacob from a strange people, Judah was made his holiness and Israel his power." Now if we look only at the letter, it signifies the exodus of the children of Israel from Egypt in the time of Moses; if at the allegory, it tells us of our redemption through Christ; if at the moral sense, it tells us of the conversion of the soul from the grief and misery of sin to a state of grace; if at the anagogical sense, it tells us of the exodus of the redeemed soul from the slavery of this corruption to the freedom of eternal glory.

E. Moore and Paget Toynbee (eds.), *Opre di Dante Alighieri* (New York, 1924), 415-16, misprints in the Latin, lines 4 and 2 from the end: *loctu* should be *luctu, existus* should be *exitus*.

Twenty years later, Teacher would be less willing to burden the pupils with this stuff, which seems to confuse the general meaning and the specialized meaning of *allegory* to little purpose, and would instead agree with Dorothy Sayers in one of her splendidly illuminating commentaries that "it is a little tiresome of Dante to have given two meanings for the same word—especially as the second, more general, meaning is the one in which we to-day always use the term 'allegorical'." Sayers, "Fourfold Interpretation of the Comedy," in *Introductory Papers on Dante* (London, 1954), 104. Indeed, Teacher could persuade himself to summary by saying "it's alighierical, and the anagoge is the alleglory." As Joyce must almost certainly have observed.

as Harold Rosenberg observed, was understood by the ancient Hindus to be one of the fifty-seven varieties of interior decoration). But maybe that is but a reflection of the fact that genius is exceedingly rare at all times, and possibly even in our sad present some great artist will illuminate and transform the world again by his unique vision. All the same, to be a good reader of Proust it will be necessary to take with seriousness—the seriousness at any rate of poetry—the thought, however silly to sense and reasonableness, that art offers an image for the redemption of suffering humanity.

I return now to say why I think the composition of Proust's book should be thought of musically—by analogy, indeed, but an analogy which can be stated in some little detail.

There is an ideal of art that mostly remains just that, an ideal, and honored chiefly in the breach. It is that somehow the art work should be omnipresent to itself, that the whole should, in some way impossible to describe, inhabit each of the parts. Perhaps it is in music that this ideal comes nearest to being realized; though if you remember one or two of the pictures by Vasarely exhibited in the library a week ago you will be able to recognize something similar in the visual arts: how a subject may be represented entirely by the aid of one or two motifs: a pair of zebras, for example—recognizable though he didn't call them zebras—against a landscape, and both zebras and background built up entirely of the alternation of black bands and white bands.

The illustration on the blackboard presents the first few measures of one of J. S. Bach's Sinfonias, or "Three Part Inventions," no. 9 in F Minor. These are contrapuntal works generally speaking in canon, where each of the three voices gets the theme in turn. What I want you to see about it is how in a quite literal sense it is always present to itself, though under various disguises and variations. It is clear that the three-note figure in the treble that begins the piece is the theme. Very well. But observe that the little arabesque figure in the bass in measure 3 is also the theme, compressed and decorated, and is followed by a form of the theme inverted and also a bit dressed-up yet recognizable. When you have seen this you may marvel, not only at the composer's skill, but also at the skill with which we, even if untrained in music, are able to

Sinfonia 9.

pick up instantly and as though automatically the likeness that is invariant under all transformations. For example, the chromatic figure descending in the bass may now be heard, though it is one of Bach's commonest ways of using the third voice in fugues, as thematic; and even the conventional cadence of the bass at the end of the second measure begins to appear as an inversion of the motif. Now this small but profound piece of music goes on for thirty-five measures in which it is fair to say there is nothing that cannot be traced to the little three-note figure that is its subject and its only subject. In this way you may see how it can be said that a piece of music is about itself, and that the whole of it is present at every instant. For a more extended example, and one in which even more transformations of the theme occur, I recommend to you, if you know music, the Fugue in D-sharp Minor, the eighth one in the First Book of the *Well-Tempered Clavier*. This is one of our ways of imitating Nature by showing how in our works as in hers the oak is contained in the acorn.

Returning now to Proust, the other term of my analogy, I shall try to show very briefly for now the way in which his style of composition is such that in many instances the same atoms, so to

say, go to form very different structures; and I will contend, leaving
the full demonstration for another day, that his way of composing
certain paragraphs is in some sense a key to the composition of his
entire work.

I pause to note that while I came upon this idea myself, some
of its separate parts have naturally been remarked by other observ-
ers. Professor Hindus, for example, notes Proust's preoccupation
with what he calls the art comparison—the way in which, for
instance, the pregnant serving maid reminds him of Giotto's
Charity, or Odette reminds Swann of a girl by Botticelli. Roger
Shattuck has written a whole little book, called *Proust's Binoculars,*
devoted to the frequent appearance of optical instruments throughout the novel. And it may be, for I am not up on the whole or even
a large part of the literature about Proust, that some other writer
has seen and described the whole of what I'm after. I didn't make
an essay about my results, partly because it is a subject that requires
vast amounts of quotation, which would make it clumsy to read,
but partly also because I did not understand the sense of what I had
seen.

> For a long time I used to go to bed early. Sometimes, when I had put out my
> candle, my eyes would close so quickly that I had not even time to say "I'm
> going to sleep." And half an hour later the thought that it was time to go to
> sleep would awaken me; I would try to put away the book which, I imagined,
> was still in my hands, and to blow out the light; I had been thinking all the
> time, while I was asleep, of what I had just been reading, but my thoughts
> had run into a channel of their own, until I myself seemed actually to have
> become the subject of my book: a church, a quartet, the rivalry between
> François I and Charles V. This impression would persist for some moments
> after I was awake; it did not disturb my mind, but it lay like scales upon my
> eyes and prevented them from registering the fact that the candle was no
> longer burning. Then it would begin to seem unintelligible, as the thoughts
> of a former existence must be to a reincarnate spirit; the subject of my book
> would separate itself from me, leaving me free to choose whether I would
> return and I would be astonished to find myself in a state of darkness, pleasant
> and restful enough for the eyes, and even more, perhaps, for my mind, to
> which it appeared incomprehensible, without a cause, a matter dark indeed
> (I, 3).

Consider the opening paragraph, and what sorts of things are constated in it. I make out the following categories, which I give each with an example, but I shan't insist that mine is the only way of breaking things down:

1. quality of air, quality of light. Darkness and the candle.

2. reference to art. The book he is reading; a church; a quartet.

3. religion and myth. Church, reincarnate spirit, former existence.

4. history. The rivalry between François I and Charles V.

5. disguise. I became the subject of my book.

6. way of seeing, deceptiveness of sight. Scales upon my eyes . . . begin to seem unintelligible.

7. travel. Whistling of trains . . . traveler.

8. nature, most often flowers, but here the note of a bird in the forest.

9. mechanical device. The train would do, but as the device involved in the cluster is typically an optical instrument, something that produces effects on seeing, I prefer to wait for the next page, where "kaleidoscope" comes in.

10. name. François I and Charles V.

If this seems arbitrary, look now at the couple of paragraphs beginning at the bottom of page 7, the famous description of the magic lantern.

At Combray, as every afternoon ended, long before the time when I should have to go up to bed, and to lie there, unsleeping, far from my mother and grandmother, my bedroom became the fixed point on which my melancholy and anxious thoughts were centered. Some one had had the happy idea of giving me, to distract me on evenings when I seemed abnormally wretched, a magic lantern, which used to be set on top of my lamp while we waited for dinner-time to come: in the manner of the master builders and glass-painters of gothic days it substituted for the opaqueness of my walls an impalpable iridescence, supernatural phenomena of many colors, in which legends were depicted, as on a shifting and transitory window. But my sorrows were only increased, because this change of lighting destroyed, as nothing else could have done, the customary impression I had formed of my room, thanks to which the room itself, but for the torture of having to go to bed in it, had become quite endurable. For now I no longer recognised it, and I became uneasy, as though I were in a room in some hotel or furnished lodging, in a place where I had just arrived, by train, for the first time.

Riding at a jerky trot, Golo, his mind filled with an infamous design, issued from the little three-cornered forest which dyed dark-green the slope of a convenient hill, and advanced by leaps and bounds towards the castle of poor Geneviève de Brabant. This castle was cut off short by a curved line which was in fact the circumference of one of the transparent ovals in the slides which were pushed into position through a slot in the lantern. It was only the wing of a castle, and in front of it stretched a moor on which Geneviève stood, lost in contemplation, wearing a blue girdle. The castle and the moor were yellow, but I could tell their colour without waiting to see them, for before the slides made their appearance the old-gold sonorous name of Brabant had given me an unmistakable clue. Golo stopped for a moment and listened sadly to the little speech read aloud by my great-aunt, which he seemed perfectly to understand, for he modified his attitude with a docility not devoid of a degree of majesty, so as to conform to the indications given in the text; then he rode away at the same jerky trot. And nothing could arrest his slow progress. If the lantern were moved I could still distinguish Golo's horse advancing across the window-curtains, swelling out with their curves and diving into their folds. The body of Golo himself, being of the same supernatural substance as his steed's, overcame all material obstacles—everything that seemed to bar his way—by taking each as it might be a skeleton and embodying it in himself: the door-handle, for instance, over which, adapting itself at once, would float invincibly his red cloak or his pale face, never losing its nobility or its melancholy, never shewing any sign of trouble at such a transubstantiation (I, 7–8).

1. impalpable iridescence . . . colors, old-gold sonorous name

2. master-builders and glass painters

3. myth: the tale of Golo and Geneviève. legends . . .

4. gothic days, merovingian past, etc.

5. the furnishings, even the door-handle, are disguised—as Golo on his horse.

6. the whole description is about this.

7. a place where I had just arrived, by train, for the first time.

8. forest, moor

9. magic lantern

10. Combray, Golo, Geneviève . . . the old-gold sonorous name of Brabant

For the present I shall but assert that this constatation takes place ever so often, and that it represents for me, at the very least, something I spoke of before: the artist's own individual variation of what Kant called the transcendental *a priori* unity of apperception, that mysterious force that intervenes between sense and thought so that the latter may receive into itself not mere separate sensations and not mere electric and chemical modifications of the neurones, but a world.

IV

Last time I spoke of the method of composition, saying why I thought it might properly be called *musical*. There will be many later opportunities of returning to and developing our demonstrations of this subject; today, however, I wish to talk rather about the thematic content of the first section, and say something of how it foreshadows, or, indeed, one might say, *predestines* the preoccupations of the entire work. For just as Proust tells this part of the story from a double point of view, that of the narrator after the end and that of the child before the beginning,* so it appears that quite possibly he wrote his book as it were from both ends at once; in a letter of 1920, at any rate, he says, "The last page of my book was written several years ago" (Fowlie, 63).

I imagine that to a first reading these thirty pages may sound like random memories—certainly they don't sound much like novel writing!—and not very remarkable. Perhaps some of you sympathized in reading with the impatience of that early publisher's reader who wondered why we should have to hear at such length about how a gentleman turns over in bed. Yet if you can grasp firmly what it is that happens in this introduction I think you will find that ever so much of the novel proliferates from the two nuclear

---

*Gaining thereby immense power over our feelings. A fanciful comparison: the opening of Beethoven's Sonata op. 106, after the fanfare, when in introducing the theme the treble ascends while the bass descends, creating an effect of vast, echoing space between, before they come back together.

sources, the good-night kiss and the madeleine, and that in retrospect you will acknowledge with what art the author has brought his universe into being. For the episode of the good-night kiss evokes one half of the world of the novel, love and its sufferings, and society, while that of the madeleine evokes the other half, involuntary memory leading on to art and its powers, and to imagination redeeming what is lost.

THE GOOD-NIGHT KISS. This center gathers to itself all that in the novel is consequent on one's dependence on others, one's weakness and loneliness, which seems at first to be greatest in the case of a child among grown-ups; but in truth the situation of the child is but our first image for the way in which Marcel, like all of us, remains dependent during most of his life, on lovers, on friends, on people in society, even on servants.

ISOLATION. Marcel is an only child (Proust had a brother), maybe the onlyest child there ever was. His isolation has a multiple power and function: in one aspect it belongs to sorrow, loneliness in strange rooms, discomfort, insomnia, and so on; in another, to comfort in seclusion (two instances of this: I, 6, rooms in winter; and the bathroom (10) where he takes refuge from cowardice, and which is associated not only with the usual functions but also with reading, dreaming, crying, and masturbating); while in a third aspect isolation is associated with spying and secret power, as at page 25 when he hides at the window to look from secret at the family below. This third aspect marks two critically important scenes later on: his observation of Mlle. Vinteuil and her friend at Montjouvain, and his similar witness from hiding of the encounter between Charlus and Jupien in the Hotel de Guermantes; both of them homosexual episodes, in which he plays the part of a voyeur. (But of course we could say that such shifts represent the embarrassment natural to first person narration—how do you get the narrator into position for receiving secret information necessary to the novel?—and no less innocent, or no more, than Jim Hawkins' hiding in a barrel to overhear the conspirators in *Treasure Island*. Though I note on the other side that Marcel the narrator is quite capable of being omniscient as to things he could not at all have known.

> . . . M. de Bréauté, when he asked himself who I could be, felt that the field of explanation was very wide. For a moment the name of M. Widor flashed before his mind, but he decided that I was not old enough to be an organist, and M. Widor not striking enough to be "asked out." It seemed on the whole more plausible to regard me simply as the new Attaché at the Swedish Legation of whom he had heard, and he was preparing to ask me for the latest news of King Oscar . . . (I, 1025–26).)

One remembers also, about isolation in a room, that the child's situation remarkably duplicates Proust's own situation while writing the novel: alone in his soundproofed, fumigated room, sending out inquiries for information as to what hat so and so wore to a garden party twenty years before, spying on the world, etc. And it is significant, perhaps, that the madeleine, which caused sunken worlds to rise again and become visible, is primarily associated with Tante Léonie, another recluse and spy on the doings of Combray. Now it seems to me that the power of a novelist will consist, not in what strange and wondrous things he tells, but rather in how much significance he is able to make emanate, by artistry, from the things he tells. I shall try briefly to put before you what seems to flow from this center, the mother's kiss which is described as the Host, the viaticum.

The kiss is a ritual, and thus belongs to custom and habit; it confers a religious reassurance, "the power to sleep." But there come occasions when this ritual is abrogated in favor of another; when there are guests there is no kiss. But the only guest is Swann, who enters the novel as the unconscious agent of Marcel's deprivation, and the child thinks that his sending a letter by Françoise to his mother would have appeared ridiculous to Swann; but the narrator tells us that in fact Swann had suffered in exactly the same manner for many years:

> As for the agony through which I had just passed, I imagined that Swann would have laughed heartily at it if he had read my letter and had guessed its purpose; whereas, on the contrary, as I was to learn in due course, a similar anguish had been the bane of his life for many years, and no one perhaps could have understood my feelings at that moment so well as himself; to him, that anguish which lies in knowing that the creature one adores is in some

place of enjoyment where oneself is not and cannot follow—to him that anguish came through Love, to which it is in a sense predestined, by which it must be equipped and adapted; but when, as had befallen me, such an anguish possesses one's soul before Love has yet entered into one's life, then it must drift, awaiting Love's coming, vague and free, without precise attachment, at the disposal of one sentiment to-day, of another to-morrow, of filial piety or affection for a comrade (I, 23–24).

And this knowledge introduces a meditation on the lover's dependence on intermediaries—servants, friends—who alas are all too often powerless to help him. This connection of Marcel and Swann remains a powerful emblem throughout the novel, for the long *nouvelle Un Amour de Swann*, though complete in itself, also shadows forth Marcel's sufferings first from Gilberte but then from Albertine; so that Swann in certain respects becomes the model for Marcel's life, with the critical differences that Swann marries whereas Marcel does not, Swann remains caught in society for all his learning and sophistication, whereas Marcel does not, and Marcel becomes the artist that Swann does not.

It is doubtful that Proust read Freud—certainly I remember no reference to Freud—yet the classic Oedipal situation is plain to be seen in this episode. Swann, in unconsciously preventing the kiss, is acting as the father; but behind Swann there is the real father, whose wrath at any emotional display on Marcel's part is much to be feared (it is to be remarked, however, that after this scene the father disappears, his part so thoroughly taken over by Swann that Marcel falls in love from a distance with his wife and more intimately with his daughter). In mother and father, seconded by grandmother and Swann, we can see how the matter of being kissed good night involves two moralities—the rule of law, custom, habit, and the rule of caprice—which might be associated with the two ways as well, the bourgeois way as over against the aristocratic way. Mother and grandmother operate by rule and in a principled manner, father pays no heed to "principles," and "in his sight there were no such things as 'rights of man' " (I, 28). Tonight, though, this difference works unexpectedly and dramatically in the child's favor; the father sends the mother to stay in the child's room; and this, coming instead of the expected and awaited punishment, produces effects that condition the narrator's entire view and conduct of life: "when I had just committed a sin so deadly that I was waiting to be banished from the household, my parents gave me a far greater concession than I should ever have won as the reward of a good action" (I, 28–29). The child's weakness is encouraged and rewarded, where his strength would not have been. And the power of this small drama, reverberant with so many themes of the whole vast work, is summed up in a marvelous passage of regret:

> Many years have passed since that night. The wall of the staircase, up which I had watched the light of his candle gradually climb, was long ago demolished. And in myself, too, many things have perished which, I imagined, would last for ever, and new structures have arisen, giving birth to new sorrows and new joys which in those days I could not have foreseen, just as now the old are difficult of comprehension. It is a long time, too, since my father has been able to tell Mamma to "Go with the child." Never again will such hours be possible for me. But of late I have been increasingly able to catch, if I listen attentively, the sound of the sobs which I had the strength to control in my father's presence, and which broke out only when I found myself alone with Mamma. Actually, their echo has never ceased: it is only because life is now growing more and more quiet round about me that I hear them afresh, like those convent bells which are so effectively drowned during the day by the noises of the streets that one would suppose them to have been stopped for ever, until they sound out again through the silent evening air. . . .
>
> I ought then to have been happy; I was not. It struck me that my mother had just made a first concession which must have been painful to her, that it was a first step down from the ideal she had formed for me, and that for the first time she, with all her courage, had to confess herself beaten. It struck me that if I had just scored a victory it was over her; that I had succeeded, as sickness or sorrow or age might have succeeded, in relaxing her will, in altering her judgement; that this evening opened a new era, must remain a black date in the calendar. . . . her anger would have been less difficult to endure than this new kindness which my childhood had not known; I felt that I had with an impious and secret finger traced a first wrinkle upon her soul and made the first white hair shew upon her head (I, 29–30).

Having seen this, we can see also that the sense of the good-night kiss is exactly the same as the sense of the madeleine episode; both are about the unexpected and undeserved superiority of grace over works. In the first, morality produces unhappiness while sin produces bliss, though that bliss is marred in its selfish delight by equally selfish guilt. In the second, after conscious intellection and voluntary memory have failed to return one to the truth and feeling of one's past, mere accident does so.

For the remarkable last part of this overture is introduced by a description of the weakness of what we ordinarily call remembering—"the pictures which that kind of memory shows us of the past preserve nothing of the past itself" (I, 33). And only many years later, by the accident of the little cake dipped in tea, does the past return alive and rich and whole, with its power of giving "exquisite pleasure":

> I feel that there is much to be said for the Celtic belief that the souls of those whom we have lost are held captive in some inferior being, in an animal, in a plant, in some inanimate object, and so effectively lost to us until the day (which to many never comes) when we happen to pass by the tree or to obtain possession of the object which forms their prison. Then they start and tremble, they call us by our name, and as soon as we have recognised their voice the spell is broken. We have delivered them: they have overcome death and return to share our life (I, 34).

This experience with the madeleine is the first, and naturally most famous, of a series of such things. How many depends on which ones you count as fully representing the experience. Fowlie, for instance, speaks of six or seven, while Samuel Beckett lists eleven. At any rate, the five most important come all at once, at the beginning of the end, and one of them is actually embodied in George Sand's *François le Champi*, already mentioned in the "Overture." Characteristically, however, it is embodied not in the novel itself but in the color and feel of its binding. For it is notable that all or practically all of the experiences involving the full revelation are experiences of the more primitive and illiterate senses, here taste, and at the end, touch, texture, sound (noise), with one in the middle evoked by a smell. This is probably because these senses have no developed articulation in language. Sound, of course, is articulated as music; but noise is not, and we probably have as little language for the discrimination of various sorts of noise as for the discrimination of tastes, colors,* smells, textures. The objects expe-

---

*Merriam-Webster's *Unabridged Dictionary of the English Language* illustrates 152 colors in the spectrum (half a dozen of them haven't even been named!), but the language we actually use about what we actually see is not very delicate: how many greens are lumped

rienced, then, by these underdeveloped senses, may retain an archaic power over our feelings for the reason that in civilized life we substitute wherever possible language for experience, and while language is a wonderful power there is also a way in which it may be seen as a deprivation of the senses and an impoverishment of experience. For language is not only a way of exploring experience, but also a defense against the too-many and too-much of things: how many snowflakes go to make up the simple statement, It is snowing.

Observe, too, how Proust's sensory preoccupations in his descriptive paragraphs attempt to extend the reach and probe of language to identify sensations that other writers scarcely attempt to deal with: qualities of air and light, for example, and the relation of such qualities through association with the qualities of certain paintings, historical periods, legends, names.

As the mother's gift of herself came to the child by a surprising overthrow of customary expectations, and bliss arose from deepest sorrow, so the world opened by the madeleine, also the mother's gift, incidentally, is a surprise, something conferred by mere chance in the midst of the depression—"weary after a dull day with the prospect of a depressing morrow"—offered by consciousness and intellection. Observe, however, that though the gift comes about by accident it remains to Marcel to decide what to make of it, and though he thinks as hard as he can for several pages, and we see him come near the answer, he does not reach it—"I did not yet know and must long postpone the discovery of why this memory made me so happy" (I, 36). The road to the understanding of it is the course itself of the novel.

SOME THOUGHTS ON "COMBRAY." It opens on a series of chords of imagery such as we have already remarked. In the first paragraph you have a description of the town keyed to qualities of light and dark, compared to painting, associated with religion in several ways, associated with travel (the railway), with legend (Geneviève and Golo), full of history and depth in time, beginning

together when we say the garden is green. When color first came to TV, a friend invited me to watch a golf tournament, but not really to watch it; no, he had me stand by the window while he fiddled with the knobs and asked periodically, "Does that look more like grass?"

with a name and ending with a name, involving a reference to an optical instrument (magic lantern). Disguise (one of you suggested transformation is the better word, and I think you are right) and way of seeing seem combined: "painted in colors so different. . . . seem to me now more insubstantial than the projections of my magic lantern" (I, 37).

Aunt Léonie introduced:

> In the next room I could hear my aunt talking quietly to herself. She never spoke save in low tones, because she believed that there was something broken in her head and floating loose there, which she might displace by talking too loud; but she never remained for long, even when alone, without saying something, because she believed that it was good for her throat, and that by keeping the blood there in circulation it would make less frequent the chokings and other pains to which she was liable . . . (I, 38).

Talking and not talking, waking and sleeping; her belief that there was something loose in her head which might be displaced by too-loud talking; her bedside table; pepsin and vespers; her reading aloud the street life of Combray. . . . it is tempting to see in the portrait of this nutty old recluse a parody of the novelist himself.

Another chord of images describes the preparation of the tea associated with the madeleine:

> After waiting a minute, I would go in and kiss her; Françoise would be making her tea; or, if my aunt were feeling "upset," she would ask instead for her "tisane," and it would be my duty to shake out of the chemist's little package on to a plate the amount of lime-blossom required for infusion in boiling water. The drying of the stems had twisted them into a fantastic trellis, in whose intervals the pale flowers opened, as though a painter had arranged them there, grouping them in the most decorative poses. The leaves, which had lost or altered their own appearance, assumed those instead of the most incongruous things imaginable, as though the transparent wings of flies or the blank sides of labels or the petals of roses had been collected and pounded, or interwoven as birds weave the material for their nests. A thousand trifling little details—the charming prodigality of the chemist—details which would have been eliminated from an artificial preparation, gave me, like a book in which one is astonished to read the name of a person whom one knows, the pleasure of finding that these were indeed real lime-blossoms, like those I had seen, when coming from the train, in the Avenue de la Gare, altered, but only because they were not imitations but the very same blossoms, which had grown old. And as each new character is merely a metamorphosis from something older, in these little grey balls I recognized

green buds plucked before their time; but beyond all else the rosy, moony, tender glow which lit up the blossoms among the frail forest of stems from which they hung like little golden roses—marking, as the radiance upon an old wall still marks the place of a vanished fresco, the difference between those parts of the tree which had and those which had not been "in bloom"— shewed me that these were petals which, before their flowering-time, the chemist's package had embalmed on warm evenings of spring. That rosy candle-light was still their colour, but half-extinguished and deadened in the diminished life which was now theirs, and which may be called the twilight of a flower. Presently my aunt was able to dip in the boiling infusion, in which she would relish the savour of dead or faded blossoms, a little madeleine, of which she would hold out a piece to me when it was sufficiently soft (I, 39).

But it is impossible for me to comment on all or even most of the things that strike me about this very quiet hundred or so pages. I must select, and hope to select things that are essential.

There are three main divisions. First, the evocation of the town of Combray as promised by the taste of the madeleine. Second, the walk called Swann's Way. Third, the walk in the opposite direction called the Guermantes Way.

I said that this is a quiet book, containing much that is dreamy and undramatic; yet its tensions are very real ones, and now and again they flash out, though perhaps they do so more recognizably at one's second and subsequent readings than at the first. It is as it were an expansion of the themes of the "Overture"; and I can well imagine that Proust's method of large-scale construction is chiefly by expanding and filling in of interstices, correcting of former impressions; it might best be symbolized by the comparison, in the last paragraph of the "Overture," of the effect of the madeleine to the Japanese flowers:

And just as the Japanese amuse themselves by filling a porcelain bowl with water and steeping in it little crumbs of paper which until then are without character or form, but, the moment they become wet, stretch themselves and bend, take on color and distinctive shape, become flowers or houses or people, permanent and recognisable, so in that moment all the flowers in our garden and in M. Swann's park, and the water-lilies on the Vivonne and the good folk of the village and their little dwellings and the parish church and the whole of Combray and of its surroundings, taking their proper shapes and growing solid, sprang into being, town and gardens alike, from my cup of tea (I, 36).

Again, it is as if all the parts of the book exist together, implicitly, all at once, in the realm of idea, only waiting to be unfolded in the realm of time.

The theme of "Combray" is, most largely, childhood memories and the power of impressions early formed over one's receipt of later experience. A little more narrowly characterized, the theme plays over such questions as How do things get their names? (etymologies already brought up by the curate, at page 79, a motif to be vastly elaborated by Brichot the academician a long time later), and How do things come to resemble their names? or Do things really resemble their names? And how do we know when we are really experiencing something we have heard of or read about? Typically, for Proust (and his readers) the real experience of something anticipated in terms of the glamor of its name is a terrible disappointment: so when the narrator, having heard from Legrandin and Swann about Balbec cathedral, and having imagined it fronting the surge of the sea and shrouded in fog, as well as Persian in style, actually goes to Balbec he finds the cathedral in a market square a dozen miles from the sea. His first visit to the theater to hear Berma is a similar letdown. In "Combray" a major instance is Marcel's first sight of the Duchesse de Guermantes:

> My disappointment was immense. It arose from my not having borne in mind, when I thought of Mme. de Guermantes, that I was picturing her to myself in the colours of a tapestry or a painted window, as living in another century, as being of another substance than the rest of the human race. Never had I taken into account that she might have a red face, a mauve scarf like Mme. Sazerat; and the oval curve of her cheeks reminded me so strongly of people whom I had seen at home that the suspicion brushed against my mind (though it was immediately banished) that this lady in her creative principle, in the molecules of her physical composition, was perhaps not substantially the Duchesse de Guermantes, but that her body, in ignorance of the name that people had given it, belonged to a certain type of femininity which included, also, the wives of doctors and tradesmen (I, 134).

If this is a problem for all of us as children, as well as later on, it is particularly a problem for Marcel who already hopes to become a writer. Its relation to novel-writing is described toward the beginning, in a remarkable passage of analysis of "real people" in fiction and elsewhere, which unites in a central thought the two realms of social life and art:

> These were the events which took place in the book I was reading. It is true that the people concerned in them were not what Françoise would have called "real people." But none of the feelings which the joys or misfortunes of a "real" person awaken in us can be awakened except through a mental picture of those joys or misfortunes; and the ingenuity of the first novelist lay in his understanding that, as the picture was the one essential element in the complicated structure of our emotions, so that simplification of it which consisted in the suppression, pure and simple, of "real" people would be a decided improvement. A "real" person, profoundly as we may sympathise with him, is in a great measure perceptible only through our senses, that is to say, he remains opaque, offers a dead weight which our sensibilities have not the strength to lift. If some misfortune comes to him, it is only in one small section of the complete idea we have of him that we are capable of feeling any emotion; indeed it is only in one small section of the complete idea he has of himself that he is capable of feeling any emotion either. The novelist's happy discovery was to think of substituting for those opaque sections, impenetrable by the human spirit, their equivalent in immaterial sections, things, that is, which the spirit can assimilate to itself. After which it matters not that the actions, the feelings of this new order of creatures appear to us in the guise of truth, since we have made them our own, since it is in ourselves that they are happening, that they are holding in thrall, while we turn over, feverishly, the pages of the book, our quickened breath and staring eyes (I, 64).

And toward the end of this book the answer, the resolution of the question of art, comes up in the vision and description of the steeples of Martinville: "And presently their outlines and their sunlit surface, as though they had been a sort of rind, were stripped apart; a little of what they had concealed from me became apparent; an idea came into my head which had not existed for me a moment earlier, framed itself in words in my head; and the pleasure with which the first sight of them, just now, had filled me was so much enhanced that, over powered by a sort of intoxication, I could no longer think of anything but them" (I, 139).

The dreamy and meditative descriptions of which the book is mostly composed are broken several times by episodes of a certain violence. One of these is Marcel's visit to Uncle Adolphe who is entertaining a lady in pink, an actress. Marcel is fascinated and charmed, though not until many years after does he realize this lady in pink was Odette de Crécy who became Mme. Swann. But the scene has a bitter sequel; charmed with his own importance Marcel gives his parents a full description of the visit which makes the parents break off relations with the uncle; and by a fateful accident of social inadequacy the narrator appears a few days later to do the same thing: "Beside the immensity of these emotions I considered that merely to raise my hat to him would be incongruous and petty, and might make him think that I regarded myself as bound to show him no more than the commonest form of courtesy. I decided to abstain from so inadequate a gesture, and turned my head away. My uncle thought that, in doing so, I was obeying my parents' orders; he never forgave them; and though he did not die until many years later, not one of us ever set eyes on him again" (I, 60).

Another such episode is the revelation that Legrandin is a snob ("a Saint Sebastian of snobbery," I, 99). This revelation is produced by physiological means:

> Legrandin's face shewed an extraordinary zeal and animation; he made a profound bow, with a subsidiary backward movement which brought his spine sharply up into a position behind its starting-point, a gesture in which he must have been trained by the husband of his sister, Mme. de Cambremer. This rapid recovery caused a sort of tense muscular wave to ripple over Legrandin's hips, which I had not supposed to be so fleshy; I cannot say why, but this undulation of pure matter, this wholly carnal fluency, with not the least hint in it of spiritual significance, this wave lashed to a fury by the wind of an assiduity, an obsequiousness of the basest sort, awoke my mind suddenly to the possibility of a Legrandin altogether different from the one whom we knew (I, 95).

That is, people reveal themselves somehow anyhow, and after that it scarcely matters what they say they are doing, one has seen what they are really doing ("This is not to say that Legrandin was anything but sincere when he inveighed against snobs," I, 99). And a third revelation is the famous one at Montjouvain, where the narrator sees from a place of concealment Mlle. Vinteuil's homosexual play with her friend and the desecration of the dead father's picture:

> And yet I have since reflected that if M. Vinteuil had been able to be present at this scene, he might still, and in spite of everything, have continued to believe in his daughter's soundness of heart, and that he might even, in so

doing, have been not altogether wrong. It was true that in all Mlle. Vinteuil's actions the appearance of evil was so strong and so consistent that it would have been hard to find it exhibited in such completeness save in what is nowadays called a "sadist"; it is behind the footlights of a Paris theatre, and not under the homely lamp of an actual country house, that one expects to see a girl leading her friend on to spit upon the portrait of a father who had lived and died for nothing and no one but herself; and when we find in real life a desire for melodramatic effect, it is generally the "sadic" instinct that is responsible for it.

It is easy enough to see that these three crises, like so much of the reflection and memory they punctuate, have to do with how things seem and how things are, and how in the world we are to put them together. They are the dramatic peaks of this book, showing instantaneously and in action what the parts given to reverie develop more slowly and form a background for. So for Marcel the two walks the family used to take are not merely two walks, but come to represent an absolute mental distinction between one kind of thing and another:

> But, above all, I set between them, far more distinctly than the mere distance in miles and yards and inches which separated one from the other, the distance that there was between the two parts of my brain in which I used to think of them, one of those distances of the mind which time serves only to lengthen, which separate things irremediably from one another, keeping them for ever upon different planes. And this distinction was rendered still more absolute because the habit we had of never going both ways on the same day, or in the course of the same walk, but the "Méséglise way" one time and the "Guermantes way" another, shut them up, so to speak, far apart and unaware of each other's existence, in the sealed vessels—between which there could be no communication—of separate afternoons (I, 103–104).

See also the summary, returning to the thought of the mother's good-night kiss:

> But it is pre-eminently as the deepest layer of my mental soil, as firm sites on which I still may build, that I regard the Méséglise and Guermantes "ways." It is because I used to think of certain things, of certain people, while I was roaming along them, that the things, the people which they taught me to know, and these alone, I still take seriously, still give me joy. . . . And yet, because there is an element of individuality in places, when I am seized with a desire to see again the "Guermantes way," it would not be satisfied were I led to the banks of a river in which were lilies as fair, or even fairer than those in the Vivonne, any more than on my return home in the evening, at

the hour when there awakened in me that anguish which, later on in life, transfers itself to the passion of love, and may even become its inseparable companion, I should have wished for any strange mother to come in and say good night to me, though she were far more beautiful and more intelligent than my own (I, 141–42).

There is a great deal that I've left out; all consideration of, for example, Tante Léonie's death, the character of Françoise, the part played by Swann; the narrator's awakening desires and especially that for Gilberte; the first sight of the lady in white and the gentleman in white ducks, who turn out to be Mme. Swann and M. de Charlus (who was earlier said to be her lover); the character of Bloch and the rather mild antisemitism of the narrator's grandfather. But many of these persons, here passingly introduced, become major characters in a long, slow, complex drama of relationships, and it may be enough for the present to remind you of their brief appearances thus early on.

For it may be an initial disadvantage of a work like this, composed so as to approach as near as words will the condition of music, that many things don't make any particular sense upon their first appearance; many things are being prepared and lead as it were still a subterraneous life. The corresponding advantages are I think two in chief. One is fidelity to experience, to the way of experiencing as much as to particular experiences. For Proust is investigating the way in which as children we really do inherit the world and come to know about it, not the way, common to most novelists as to most people, in which we usually say we know things. As far as I know, no other novelist has devoted such care and thought to the humble foundations of the adult world that we are so often and thoughtlessly allowed to mistake for the real one. The other main advantage will be seen in the powerful effects permitted by this method of slow beginnings, in the marvelous turns of relationship and dramatic reversals and recognitions it makes possible later on.

It is in this sense that, if you read Proust at all, you must read all of Proust.

Why read Proust? Why read all of Proust?

The first question must be left to ripen toward its own answer as you read. As to the second, however, something may be said even now. A great novel is the story of a long time, or, even more simply, the story of time itself in its compound of circle and line (as in the mysterious simplicity of the phonograph needle moving toward the center even while simultaneously it follows the winding path and releases articulated sounds from its minutely varied terrain). The major effects of Proust's novel rely, much as time itself seems to rely, on causes that grow subterraneously, invisibly, until at last they erupt through the surface and begin to bloom as determinate effects. These effects are as near heart-breaking in their purity and decisiveness as anything in literature, but to experience them at all you must experience the long period of their germination.

In a sense, not much happens in the entire great work. People rise and fall in society, a whole society goes down and is replaced by another, people make love, marry, have children, die . . . but all this seems in a paradoxical way "not much" because it happens so continuously, almost as in life itself, where the form of things appears as a constant exactly and only because the material fabric of it is always changing. Proust's figure for this, or one of his figures, is the fountain of Hubert Robert.

For example: on leaving this building you will walk down the road either to the right or to the left; toward the museum and theater, or toward the library, the castle. Suppose one said to you: it will be the substance of a long life's work for you to find out that these two roads are really one and don't go in opposite directions at all but meet at the college entrance; you might reply that you have already discovered this, and that it seems to you a singularly unremarkable circumstance. Well, so would it be for you to be told now that the two ways, the two walks, of Proust's novel, seen as opposites at the beginning, are discovered to be one at the end. Unremarkable. But the poignancy of effect in this simple discovery—which I have no fear that I spoil for you by thus anticipating—comes from the vast complex of feelings and thoughts that has been all the while invisibly weaving up the fabrics of Swann's Way and the Guermantes Way until their being perceived as one way shall come to be inevitable and right, and, odd as it seems, a real discovery.

V

Having for nearly a hundred and fifty pages established his subject matter—himself—the novelist drops it completely and devotes the next hundred and fifty pages to someone else, to "a story which . . . had been told me of a love affair in which Swann had been involved before I was born" (I, 143). This seems a very strange way of proceeding, however interesting the story of Swann and Odette may be in itself. And for its compositional justification, we may have to wait quite a long time; yet it is worth pausing even now to reflect on the sense of this interruption which places a whole new novel within the novel that has just barely got started. The casual introduction of it is worth having in full:

> And so I would often lie until morning, dreaming of the old days at Combray, of my melancholy and wakeful evenings there; of other days besides, the memory of which had been more lately restored to me by the taste—by what would have been called at Combray the "perfume"—of a cup of tea; and, by an association of memories, of a story which, many years after I had left the little place, had been told me of a love affair in which Swann had been involved before I was born; with that accuracy of detail which it is easier, often, to obtain when we are studying the lives of people who have been dead for centuries than when we are trying to chronicle those of our own most intimate friends, an accuracy which it seems as impossible to attain as it seemed impossible to speak from one town to another, before we learned of the contrivance by which that impossibility has been overcome. All these memories, following one after another, were condensed into a single substance, but had not so far coalesced that I could not discern between the three strata, between my oldest, my instinctive memories, those others,

inspired more recently by a taste or "perfume," and those which were actually the memories of another, from whom I had acquired them at second hand— no fissures, indeed, no geological faults, but at least those veins, those streaks of colour which in certain rocks, in certain marbles, point to differences of origin, age, and formation (I, 143).

You observe that this passage is a subtle repetition of most of those images that we have remarked as going together to build Proust's world: the "perfume," the note on history, the mechanical "contrivance" of the telephone. The contention seems to be that by getting a great distance away from something you may see it better than you could see something close at hand; and by an implicit comparison, Marcel may be better able to view Swann's affair than his own, or that view may be an indispensable prelude to inspecting his own affair with Albertine so much later.

In the idea that one's own memories and those of others are not always distinguishable there seems to be a kind of key to the composition of the novel, which thus announces an intention of aiming rather at reality than at *realism*. Proust has very little interest in the literary convention called *realism*, for, as one of his commentators nicely observes: "Realism in fiction never corresponds to reality in life, because it presupposes an impossible point of view— that one which lacks a viewer."* What Proust is after, through, with, despite, all his keenness of observation, is magic—revelation—and what is to be revealed is, as with the good-night kiss and the madeleine, relationship, general law underlying particular action, entire worlds, rich with many lives, exfoliating from the paradigmatic case. Swann's affair is such a case, and, detailed and full though the reporting of it may be, it is still a miniature and a kind of table of contents to the entire work, which indeed in a vital sense is made to depend upon Swann, even upon the name of Swann, which for the narrator had become "almost mythological." It is still echoing at the end (which is the beginning) of the novel, where the narrator in finding his vocation acknowledges:

But if it had not been for Swann, I would not even have known the Guermantes, since my grandmother would not then have renewed her acquaintance with Mme. de Villeparisis and I would not have met Saint-

*Howard Moss, *The Magic Lantern of Marcel Proust* (New York, 1962), 37–38.

Loup and M. de Charlus, which led to my meeting the Duchesse de Guermantes and, through her, her cousin, so that it was also through Swann that I happened at this moment to be in the house of the Prince de Guermantes, where the idea of the book I was to write had just come to me suddenly—which meant that I should be indebted to Swann, not only for its subject but also for the decision to undertake it. A rather slender stem, perhaps, to support in this way the entire expanse of my life!

So that is one sort of relationship, the flowering—note the figure of the flower in the last sentence—of effects from a cause. But there is another, symbolic or associative. As in the theological study called typology, where Old Testament figures "stand for" or are the types of New Testament figures, so Swann is a type of Marcel, who from the first appears as fated to live Swann's story over again, with certain highly significant differences, as I told you in my last lecture, so that he succeeds where Swann failed.

Most novelists work by trying to give us a sense of the continuousness of their characters' lives, and this is hard enough to do because it must be done by the discontinuous means of the narration of selected moments in those lives—though we cooperate splendidly with the illusion by never pausing to doubt that the characters live offstage as well as on. Proust does this, too, of course. Yet the opposite is also part of his method: there must be also in his characters' lives discontinuities, dissociations, what he called "intermittences." The reason for this is, I think, so that we readers shall have time, shall have the experience of time, which is the experience of forgetting just as much as of remembering, and that we shall have this experience as much as possible the way we do in life, where you will observe that memory works in two ways at least: there are things we say we remember because we have never forgotten them, things we "have always known," and there are things we remember because we did forget; these latter are the ones that have power over the soul.

Pursuing the question of memory a bit further, we see too that one sort of memory, perhaps the one most responsible for our view of our own lives as continuous in time, even if the lives of others seem intermittent, is chronological: we are able, on demand—an application form, for instance—to produce a sort of history: born so and so in such a place, went to school at this and that. . . . But this sort of memory seems to make chronological sense rather at the expense of any other sort. Another memory treats temporal succession as of no particular interest or importance at all; for it, whatever of the past is accessible at all, is equally so; the near and far in time may be thought of simultaneously, and in fact this memory, genial and creative in its power of free combination of its elements, may be very close to what we mean when we speak of *imagination* as producing the art work. So that in memory itself there is a double meaning and a double possibility: of being bound to time, and of being free from time, or rather, perhaps, free *in* time. It is this second power, or Proust's sensitive awareness of it, that makes this novel possible, as the narrator seems to say in the famous last passage of it:

> If, at least, there were granted me time enough to complete my work, I would not fail to stamp it with the seal of that Time the understanding of which was this day so forcibly imposing itself upon me, and I would therein describe men—even should that give them the semblance of monstrous creatures— as occupying in Time a place far more considerable than the so restricted one allotted them in space, a place, on the contrary, extending boundlessly since, giant-like, reaching far back into the years, they touch simultaneously epochs of their lives—with countless intervening days between—so widely separated from one another in Time.

But if this power of the memory is experienced at last by the mature artist as blessed and releasing and redeeming, it must be first experienced by the lover in its horrible and demonic and torment- ing aspect; for if the project of recapturing the past, the waste of one's life, is capable of being put in such artistic form that it can appear to succeed, the equivalent attempt of the lover, to recapture the past of the beloved, is utterly doomed; and that attempt is the story of Swann in relation to Odette de Crécy, as it is also later the story of Marcel in relation to Albertine.

Even in respect to a relatively small and simple part of *A la recherche du temps perdu* I shall have to be extremely selective as to subjects for comment, trying to avoid on the one hand making mere summaries of the plot, and on the other hand trying not to explain in my own inadequate words what the author has already explained in his so adequate ones. For my first topic I return to the question of *realism*.

Though "Un Amour de Swann" is told "objectively" and in the third person, it is I think both possible and helpful to remember that at no time do we "really see" Swann or Odette as they "really are." For this story of what Swann went through is refracted through the media, first, of another narrator, unnamed, and then of Marcel in adolescence; and in some sense a great deal of what is said, in comparison with what any narrator could realistically have *known* of Swann's life and thoughts at this period, must be conditioned by the young Marcel's thoughts about sex and love.

Now the subject of sex and love, even in a post-Freudian, post-Kinsey, atmosphere, is particularly able to generate mythological fantasies, because even if we think we know how it is with ourselves, we cannot know how it is with others; and in this connection I note that both Swann and Odette are treated in a somewhat mythologizing spirit. Of Swann we are told that before his meeting with Odette he has had a large number of affairs with women ranging in class from duchesses to their cooks, and while we accept this information as best we may it is hard not to be reminded of Don Giovanni's having laid a thousand and three girls in Spain alone, according to Leporello's notebook, and we may even think, between admiration and amazement, How did he have enough time? Odette too has been and is a sexual careerist, and so intent is the novelist on revealing the multiple planes of her ultimately nonexistent personality that it begins to seem as though there is scarcely a bed in Paris she has not been in (see I, 320, where she is the subject of a brief exchange between two nameless gentlemen):

> "You know who that is? Mme. Swann! That conveys nothing to you? Odette de Crécy, then?"
>
> "Odette de Crécy! Why, I thought as much. Those great, sad eyes. . . . But I say, you know, she can't be as young as she was once, eh? I remember, I had her on the day that MacMahon went."
>
> "I shouldn't remind her of it, if I were you. She is now Mme. Swann, the wife of a gentleman in the Jockey Club, a friend of the Prince of Wales. Apart from that, though, she is wonderful still."
>
> "Oh, but you ought to have known her then; Gad, she was lovely! She lived in a very odd little house with a lot of Chinese stuff. I remember, we

were bothered all the time by the newsboys, shouting outside; in the end she made me get up and go."

First viewed by Swann as chaste, then as a woman who gives herself only where she loves, Odette is progressively revealed to the eyes of his jealousy as a *kept woman*—Swann has some comic difficulty in realizing that this epithet may be applied to Odette as much as to any other woman in the same situation—then as a great courtesan—*une grande cocotte*—then as the common garden variety tart she most likely was (according to remarks exchanged between M. Verdurin and his wife), then as sexually ambiguous and capable of Lesbian attachments, finally as a call girl employed by procuresses. She has had also a multiplicity of pasts, having been at one time the mistress of Marcel's Uncle Adolphe, having been also an actress, or at least chorus girl, under the name of Miss Sacripant (her portrait painted by Elstir brings out a certain homoerotic viciousness):

> But above all one felt that Elstir, sublimely indifferent to whatever immoral suggestion there might be in this disguise of a young actress for whom the talent with which she would play her part on the stage was doubtless of less importance than the irritant attraction which she would offer to the jaded or depraved senses of some of her audience, had on the contrary fastened upon those ambiguous points as on an aesthetic element which deserved to be brought into prominence, and which he had done everything in his power to emphasise. Along the lines of the face, the latent sex seemed to be on the point of confessing itself to be that of a somewhat boyish girl, then vanished and farther on reappeared with a suggestion rather of an effeminate youth, vicious and pensive, then fled once more to remain uncapturable. The dreamy sadness in the expression of her eyes, by the mere fact of its contrast with the accessories belonging to the world of love-making and play-acting, was not the least disturbing element in the picture. One imagined moreover that it must be feigned, and that the young person who seemed ready to submit to caresses in this provoking costume had probably thought it effective to enhance the provocation with this romantic expression of a secret longing, an unspoken grief (I, 638).

The point I mean to bring before you is that, particularly as applied to Odette, the portrayal is the result less of realism than of a literary method whose first insistence is on successive revelations, or the revelation, bit by bit, of successive personalities, or incarnations, each one of which, at first regarded as the end of the investigation, as the truth, is later *seen through*.

But this process of detective work, whose agency is the lover's jealousy, is inextricably woven up with its opposite. For Swann could not fall in love with Odette, who, we are told first and last, was not his type, until he himself had transformed her, by the disguising, quasi-artistic power of illusion, into a woman mysteriously invested with the charm of art and tradition:

> Perhaps because the abundance of impressions which he, for some time past, had been receiving—though, indeed, they had come to him rather through the channel of his appreciation of music—had enriched his appetite for painting as well, it was with an unusual intensity of pleasure, a pleasure destined to have a lasting effect upon his character and conduct, that Swann remarked Odette's resemblance to the Zipporah of that Alessandro de Mariano, to whom one shrinks from giving his more popular surname, now that "Botticelli" suggests not so much the actual work of the Master as that false and banal conception of it which has of late obtained common currency. He no longer based his estimate of the merit of Odette's face on the more or less good quality of her cheeks, and the softness and sweetness—as of carnation-petals—which, he supposed, would greet his lips there, should he ever hazard an embrace, but regarded it rather as a skein of subtle and lovely silken threads, which his gazing eyes collected and wound together, following the curving line from the skein to the ball, where he mingled the cadence of her neck with the spring of her hair and the droop of her eyelids, as though from a portrait of herself, in which her type was made clearly intelligible (I, 171).

And I think it not too much to say that the point about the futility of Swann's quest to penetrate an illusion he has himself made up is symbolically made by a negation: he falls in love with her exactly when and exactly because she is not there.

> Among all the methods by which love is brought into being, among all the agents which disseminate that blessed bane, there are few so efficacious as the great gust of agitation which, now and then, sweeps over the human spirit. For then the creature in whose company we are seeking amusement at the moment, her lot is cast, her fate and ours decided, that is the creature whom we shall henceforward love. It is not necessary that she should have pleased us, up till then, any more, or even as much as others. All that is necessary is that our taste for her should become exclusive. And that condition is fulfilled so soon as—in the moment when she has failed to meet us—for the pleasure which we were on the point of enjoying in her charming company is abruptly substituted an anxious torturing desire, whose object is the creature herself, an irrational, absurd desire, which the laws of civilised

society make it impossible to satisfy and difficult to assuage—the insensate, agonising desire to possess her (I, 177).

Much of what I am trying to put before you is summed up in the description of their first kiss, the prelude to that "act of physical possession (in which, paradoxically, the possessor possesses nothing)," where it is possible perhaps to see something of the meaning of those linked series of images whose presence we have so often noticed:

> He slipped his other hand upwards along Odette's cheek; she fixed her eyes on him with that languishing and solemn air which marks the women of the old Florentine's paintings, in whose faces he had found the type of hers; swimming at the brink of her fringed lids, her brilliant eyes, large and finely drawn as theirs, seemed on the verge of breaking from her face and rolling down her cheeks like two great tears. She bent her neck, as all their necks may be seen to bend, in the pagan scenes as well as in the scriptural. And although her attitude was, doubtless, habitual and instinctive, one which she knew to be appropriate to such moments, and was careful not to forget to assume, she seemed to need all her strength to hold her face back, as though some invisible force were drawing it down towards Swann's. And Swann it was who, before she allowed her face, as though despite her efforts, to fall upon his lips, held it back for a moment longer, at a little distance between his hands. He had intended to leave time for her mind to overtake her body's movements, to recognise the dream which she had so long cherished and to assist at its realisation, like a mother invited as a spectator when a prize is given to the child whom she has reared and loves. Perhaps, moreover, Swann himself was fixing upon these features of an Odette not yet possessed, not even kissed by him, on whom he was looking now for the last time, that comprehensive gaze with which, on the day of his departure, a traveller strives to bear away with him in memory the view of a country to which he may never return (I, 179).

What such things seem to be insisting on in such great detail is the impossibility, for human beings, of simple perception, at least to aroused feeling. We never see simply what is there; what is there serves but as the instrument whereby the richest complexes of feeling and thought and value are evoked. So the particular event, a man kissing a woman for the first time, is rendered not simply in time as it is in space, but as a meditative summing up of the entire course of their affair, where the two minds watch the two bodies fly away with each other, where the entire species is involved by means of legend and artistic representation, where in the very first moment of aroused desire regret is already present (the traveler striving to bear away with him in memory the view of a country to which he may never return), just as in the little phrase of Vinteuil's sonata love and delight are already instinct with suffering and regret—its charm is described as that of a woman seen and admired, whom Swann despaired of ever seeing again and met in a friend's house: "And it was so peculiarly itself, it had so personal a charm, which nothing else could have replaced, that Swann felt as though he had met, in a friend's drawing-room, a woman whom he had seen and admired, once, in the street, and had despaired of ever seeing her again" (I, 162).

Now if I am correct at all in describing such paragraphs composed by linked series of images as the elementary particles, so to say, of Proust's universe, present in the smallest units of being, the next step might well be to see if some of these elementary particles do not similarly enter into the large scale architectonics of the entire novel.

I said earlier that one of the categories was Nature *tout court,* but now I am willing to narrow this category down and say that the nature represented is most often *flowers.* So, beginning with Odette's orchids, I may make a little excursion backwards and forwards in the novel to see how far the ideas of flowers and flowering will take us.

For Swann, says the narrator, the substitution of "cattleya"* for "make love" has the value of his hope "that it was the possession of this woman that would emerge for him from their large and richly colored petals," and the uniqueness of *this* woman, *this* experience, is insisted on by comparing the pleasure it gives him to that of the first man "amid the flowers of the earthly paradise."

> However disillusioned we may be about women, however we may regard the possession of even the most divergent types as an invariable and monotonous experience, every detail of which is known and can be described in advance, it still becomes a fresh and stimulating pleasure if the women concerned be— or be thought to be—so difficult as to oblige us to base our attack upon some unrehearsed incident in our relations with them, as was originally for Swann

---

*Cattleya, by the way, is a variety of orchid behind whose exotic-appearing name is the more ordinary one of Cyril Connolly's uncle, a Mr. Cattley, who produced it.

the arrangement of the cattleyas. He trembled as he hoped, that evening, (but Odette, he told himself, if she were deceived by his strategem, could not guess his intention) that it was the possession of this woman that would emerge for him from their large and richly coloured petals; and the pleasure which he already felt, and which Odette tolerated, he thought, perhaps only because she was not yet aware of it herself, seemed to him for that reason— as it might have seemed to the first man when he enjoyed it amid the flowers of the earthly paradise—a pleasure which had never before existed, which he was striving now to create, a pleasure—and the special name which he was to give to it preserved its identity—entirely individual and new (I, 180).

Indeed, Odette and flowers and mythology are strongly associated, as in the beautiful desolation of the description, many years later, of the Bois de Boulogne in November (I, 321–25). The Bois is, or was, the Elysian Garden of women, in the zoological or mythological sense of the word *Garden*, the description of it and of the women to be seen in it is full of flowers and flowering trees, resonant with mythology and *in illo tempore*, the beginning of the world—"the happy days when I was young and had faith" (I, 323)—and art comparisons follow out this line: Michelangelo's *The Creation* is the key one. The narrator reverts over and over to the theme of faith: "I no longer had the faith" (I, 324), "at a time when I still had faith," (I, 325), and at last the remembrance of Mme. Swann's (Odette's) flowers sets off the melancholy peroration about time past, where the Elysian Garden has turned into the Dark Wood, the Virgilian groves, "the unpeopled vacancy of this strange forest."

I should have liked to be able to pass the rest of the day with one of those women, over a cup of tea, in a little house with dark-painted walls (as Mme. Swann's were still in the year after that in which the first part of this story ends) against which would glow the orange flame, the red combustion, the pink and white flickering of her chrysanthemums in the twilight of a November evening. . . . Alas! there was nothing now but flats decorated in the Louis XVI style, all white paint, with hortensias in blue enamel. . . . And I should have required also that they be the same women, those whose costume interested me because, at a time when I still had faith, my imagination had individualised them and had provided each of them with a legend. Alas! in the acacia-avenue—the myrtle-alley—I did see some of them again, grown old, no more now than grim spectres of what once they had been, wandering to and fro, in desperate search of heaven knew what, through the Virgilian groves. . . . large birds passed swiftly over the Bois, as over a real wood, and with shrill cries perched, one after another, on the great oaks which, beneath their Druidical crown, and with Dodonaic majesty, seemed to proclaim the unpeopled vacancy of this estranged forest, and helped me to understand how paradoxical it is to seek in reality for the pictures that are stored in one's memory, which must inevitably lose the charm that comes to them from memory itself and from their not being apprehended by the senses. . . . Remembrance of a particular form is but regret for a particular moment; and houses, roads, avenues are as fugitive, alas, as the years (I, 324–25).

This cold and hellish spectacle of the old ladies, grim spectres in the naked November woods, is a foreshadowing of the similar but vastly expanded report of the last party of the novel, where the grim spectres are presented in grim detail. So already one sees that the idea of flowers, and especially Odette's constant association with them, involves us in mythology, and the tale of Swann and Odette really may be viewed as the story of the Fall from the Earthly Paradise into the world of generation, age, suffering, sorrow, and death; nor is the story of Persephone without its resonances here, for Mme. Swann as the genius loci of the Bois de Boulogne is viewed in her passage to the past somewhat as life going underground in winter (description of Mme. Swann and her flowers as "against the grey sky" and looking out through closed windows at the falling snow, I, 324).

And when we look for them, we find these connections among girls, flowers and flower gardens, love, suffering, in a great many places in the novel. Howard Moss, in his lovely book, starts us off: "We have three gardens to begin with: the one attached to Aunt Léonie's house; the hawthorn and lilac along the Méséglise way; and the water lilies and violets that perfume the Vivonne along the Guermantes Way . . . and around that magic land, that garden from which a child is expelled—in the same way as Adam from the garden of Eden, and for much the same reason—a universe begins to expand."* And I may paraphrase a perception he has a moment later: every garden in the novel is not only Eden, but Gethsemane as well.

Throughout *A la recherche*, girls are associated with flowers: the little band is *les jeunes filles en fleurs,* and associated with the

*Moss, *Magic Lantern*, 21.

flowering hawthorn especially, the same flowers among which Marcel first saw Gilberte, and whose presence on the altar in Holy Week he has so particularly remarked. And many more examples might be cited to show the constancy of this relation, wherein by the mediation of the thought of flowers girls become goddesses to be adored.

So flowers and flowering relate to love and desire and youth, because they are a means to the imagination, perhaps by being so superfluous in their beauty, and so useless for anything but to be looked at, smelled, and loved. But we have seen too this morning how flowering is the metaphor Marcel uses about attributing his work to Swann—a rather slender stem, he says; and it is also preeminently his figure for artistic creation, as in the flowering of Combray from the cup of tea.

VI

Proust's Society, a question of composition (its and his). The novelist and the criminal, said William Troy in an essay on Balzac, are alike in one respect: both are makers of plots.

This morning I shall take a little time simply to marvel, and invite you to marvel, at the immense achievement which is Proust's book. We readers do not, perhaps, do very much marveling; our tribute to an author may be just that, our not seeing anything remarkable in what he has done: why yes, we say, certainly; that *is* the world, what's so wonderful about that? It is only if we ourselves attempt literary composition that we get an appalled idea of the spiritual pain and pains to be taken in making up a world that shall look something like the real world and, much more to the point, give a revelation of certain of its laws. Otherwise, it is between the author and ourselves as between God and the atheist, as Proust himself has said: the greatest tribute to the Creator is the atheist, who sees the creation as so perfect and complete in itself as to have required no maker (I, 1015).

I shall try to witness to the marvelousness of the book in a very simple way, and by pointing to very simple things about it: scope, depth, complexity, articulation.

Its overall movement is worth considering first. It is given on a small scale in the prelude, which begins with a man in bed and ends with the flowering of a whole world, the world of Combray; well, so does the entire novel. It begins with the smallest unit of action: the man alone remembering the child alone, in bed; and it expands by marked stages to bring under its consideration something so large as the First World War and the absolute transformation of a society and a generation, the sinking of a great world into dark, defeat, death; yet all this, by the laws of composition of the work, remains within the mind of one man alone who at the end is left contemplating the world he will bring and has brought into being and seen die.

A few abstract observations may make more striking the grandeur of this achievement. If we begin by asking, How do human beings—how do we—see the world? the answer will be: by making up stories about it, or by hearing stories told about it. For the world is largely invisible. Which is to say that it is too big, too complex, too full of people and things, for any of us to see it directly; we have to take, as Einstein tells us the scientist does, synoptic and symbolic views; and we must, as Polonius tells us the plotter does, by indirections find direction out.

If we stop to ask What is a story? and How come stories are possible? we shall get in trouble far too deep for amateurs. A story is the recital of certain facts; that is to say, most uncertain facts, in that they obey mysterious laws of relation: they are bound to one another, these facts, by chronological sequence, but not only so; and they are bound to one another in relations of cause and effect, or ground and consequent, but not only so here either; for a last condition is that they are bound to one another by likenesses and patterns made of likenesses, so that one thing stands for another even while remaining itself. The story is as it were a great metaphor, a great synecdoche, a great metonymy, and, yes, to complete the series of tropes, a great irony as well—for in telling us everything it yet, after all, tells us nothing much, and leaves the world as mysterious when it's done as before it began. The story gives always both more and less than it promises: more, because of the mysterious richness that gathers around the recital of certain facts, and less because when we are drawn to expect the revelation of the truth of existence by its charms and terrors, it always excuses itself smilingly: it's only a story.

It is quite odd, the existence of stories. If you wanted to tell the story of the whole world would you begin by reading all the phone books? Unlikely. More likely that you begin: in the beginning God created the heaven and the earth (already you have a character doing something). Or you begin in the middle of nowhere: There was a man in the land of Uz whose name was Job. . . .

Truly, as Scott Fitzgerald said, if as a novelist you begin with something in particular it may if you are fortunate turn into something of universal import; but if you begin with something of universal import you will end with nothing.

Now the modern world—the nineteenth century to some extent, but the twentieth much more—puts some difficulties of a special sort in the storyteller's way: the size, complexity, and interrelatedness of the world made it harder to take simple account of, even while representative government and democratic institutions, by replacing monarchy, deprived the storyteller of a central image that made a hierarchy of relations for him, wherein family and state were one, as they are for example in *King Lear*.

But I warn myself and you to take these statements in moderation. Probably the world has been huge and complex since cities were founded and the division of labor instituted; also, if the old world looks simpler than the new it is in large part because our impression of the old world is founded almost entirely and exclusively on the stories it left to us. Moreover, it is the storyteller's art to make triumphs precisely out of difficulties. Nevertheless I think it may be said—in moderation—that something like what I have just observed at least seemed to novelists to have happened, and they responded in three ways. There were the ones who thought that modern life was too rich in itself to be handled by stories—one of the senses of the word is significantly "falsehood"—and so you had realism; there were the ones—fewer, these—who thought on the contrary that *only* the story could handle the mystery of life at all—"within our whole universe," says a character in a story by Isak Dinesen, "the story only has authority to answer that cry of heart of its characters, that one cry of heart of each of them: '*Who am I?*'" And finally there were the ones, fewest of all, the master novelists, all of them monsters as well as masters, who do both, who can handle without being corrupted the immense quantity of detail that realism demands, and at the end turn out to have been telling us all the while a simple old story about getting lost in the dark wood of the world and getting found again by some benevolent and reconciling strength belonging to world and spirit at once; as in *Ulysses* and *Finnegans Wake*; in *The Magic Mountain* and *Joseph*; in *Remembrance of Things Past*.

To return now to that novel. Our considerations thus far have chiefly centered on its loneliness and inwardness, but it is time now—being about one quarter the way through—to turn our attention to the other side, the brilliant and immense populous world that is mirrored in that lonely mind. It will be useful first to make a simple review of some of the things that have happened.

As the child Marcel grows to be a boy and a young man the circle of his awareness expands, sometimes gradually, sometimes quite suddenly and unexpectedly. And as the old man Marcel remembers this process he obeys both its law of chronological sequence—being bound to time—and the other law, that of memory, for which many experiences are equally accessible, though when they occurred they occurred in chronological sequence. So the story, double in itself, is being told as it were from both ends at once. It seems often as though someone were dreaming and interpreting his dream at the same time, so that the interpretation becomes inextricably part of the dream to be interpreted. Yet the process of expanding awareness is perfectly plain, and goes something like this:

First there is the world of the family; outside that circle everything is vague and rumorous, and it is remarkable that we receive this experience not as from a novelist, who introduces, describes, and explains his characters as they appear, but very much as Marcel himself receives his experience, sometimes vaguely and sometimes sharply outlined, but without apparent significance or relationship. Various names are mentioned without our knowing whether they will ever again enter into Marcel's or our future: Mme. de Villeparisis, who says one sentence about Swann's being a friend of "my nephews, the des Laumes." It is hundreds of pages later on, but ten years earlier in the time of the novel, that we learn who the des Laumes are—the Duc and Duchesse de Guermantes—and several hundred pages later and several years later in the time of the novel that we meet again Mme. de Villeparisis who, because of having been at school with Marcel's grandmother, becomes all at once his means of entry into at least the antechamber of the very highest society.

After the family there is the childhood world: Combray, provincial and quiet, yet fuller of event than the family circle, and more populous. Again we meet people whose significance is utterly closed to us, just as it would be in our own lives: a man and a woman seen at a distance are Mme. Swann and M. de Charlus, but who are they to us? A girl seen framed among hawthorn in flower turns out to be Gilberte, but only a long time later.

After "Combray" the world enlarges itself suddenly and immensely, but also vicariously and as if in anticipation, as Marcel repeats the story he has heard about Swann and Odette. This apparent interruption to the continuity of the process of growing up, or growing out into society, is an imitation and foreboding of it, as we have already seen, and introduces one of the several great social groups which by the end of the novel will be seen as composing the whole world in their transformations, their courtships and marriages and other blendings with one another: the little nucleus, the clan, of Mme. Verdurin and her husband; a bourgeois group, but much wealthier and more widely cultivated, or sophisticated, than Marcel's family, its members make up for being excluded from the aristocracy's parties by being, or pretending to be, more "interesting"—more liberal, livelier, and preoccupied with "the higher things," though always, it should be noted, after a good meal.

The Verdurins and their little circle make a good illustration of the method of composition. For while they seem to be introduced as a comic foil to the unhappy love affair and an occasion for satire all on their own, a good many things also are set in motion—as almost always, in Proust, in slow motion—which will not produce their revelations for years and, again, a thousand and more pages. The Verdurins, when we meet them, are on the way up but at the beginning of the climb. They already have money, bags of money, and their fortunes will represent the way in which the world is transformed as the power of money replaces the power of ancient lineage and a great name. In fact, Mme. Verdurin, by one of those supreme ironies whose essence is that they seem to happen imperceptibly, over a long time, succeeds in realizing her great ambition of being at the very top of society exactly by pulling it down: she becomes Princesse de Guermantes by marrying the Prince after they have both been widowed. But by that time—shattered by the Great War, another manifestation perhaps of the power of money—that society matters no more, it belongs to the past.

As they climb the social ladder, so they bring Swann down. For it is at their house that he meets the slightly disreputable woman whom he presently marries, after which it is the main ambition of Swann's remaining life—his love affair, so often compared to a disease, is replaced as it were by disease itself—that his wife and daughter should be received by his great friends the Guermantes, an ambition condemned to failure while he lived but accomplished as by metamorphosis after his death, as Odette remarries, this time to de Forcheville, and Gilberte at last marries Saint-Loup, a Guermantes, by whom she has a daughter the recognition of whom constitutes for Marcel at the very end of his pilgrimage the union of Swann's Way and the Guermantes Way with which the book began.

And the depiction of the Verdurin group introduces into the social structure a new and important kind of being: the artist, and the intellectual, and the professional man, all of whom are sort of in society without quite being of it. In this category come Dr. Cottard the physician, Brichot the academician and pedant, Saniette, also a learned man, and a rather frivolous and lightweight painter called M. Biche, whom Marcel meets much later on when he has become the great painter Elstir. It is here, too, that Swann hears the sonata of Vinteuil; and if the little phrase means much to Swann, it will mean much to Marcel also; while the life of the old musician, so humble and so gifted, will come to seem to him exemplary of the holy nature of art, even as his daughter will be the occasion of much agony to him by his suspicion of her relations with Albertine.

Much more might be said on the subject of the Verdurins and

the nature of the slow drama of relationships that exfoliates itself from their Paris establishment as later from their country place La Raspelière (rented from Mme. de Cambremer). But perhaps I have told you enough to illustrate the architectural method of the Proustian revelation.

VII

DEAR PUPILS,

The troubles I am having preparing these lectures on Proust's novel are doubtless of several kinds, the first being perhaps that I am just not very good at lecturing. But there is one in particular that may be expressed by a paradox: in Proust, so little happens that one forgets so much! I imagine that you may have experienced this too, so it may be worth spending a part of this hour on trying to understand it.

In one way, it is the method of composition I have tried to describe to you that makes the trouble. When, just now, I tried to show something of the weight and import of the Verdurin circle, I could not do so by staying within the confines of "Swann in Love," but had to look a thousand and two thousand pages ahead. Perhaps some of you will have thought that I was giving away the plot, but I think I need not reproach myself with that, for you will forget so much in the course of reading that everything will come as a surprise anyhow. Or not as a surprise, but as an inevitable fulfillment. And it is to be expected that this sort of trouble will let up as more and more of the novel becomes our past, leaving less and less in our future.

But there is the other sort of difficulty, connected with the so little and so much I spoke of a moment ago. For instance, what might I have said about "Swann in Love"?

1. It tells how Swann fell in love, suffered, fell out of love. Now

that is quite true, and it is conspicuously Proust's way that his stories are incredible expansions, or flowerings, from so simple a sentence as that one. For I might enlarge my report without changing a fact in the first version.

2. It tells how Swann met Odette de Crécy at a party given by the Verdurins, fell in love with her, and after a brief happiness began to suffer jealousy both of her possible present relations with men, especially Forcheville, and of her possible past relations with men and women; after nearly dying of helpless and hopeless love, after suffering social humiliation from the Verdurins and their clan and private humiliation from the shifts to which jealousy forced him— reading her letter to Forcheville through the envelope, for instance, or spying at her window (which turned out to be the wrong window)—after all these things, and a dream which marked the severance of the Swann that loved and suffered from the new Swann that does neither, he recovers and is able to look back on the oddity of the experience.

3. In a third version I might bring in, without falsifying the first or the second, some other items, all as well known to you as the ones already summarized: the exact nature of the Verdurins and their guests with respect to social rank; the party at the Marquise de Sainte Euverte's, Swann's friendship with the Princesse des Laumes at a social level which Odette could not hope to attain (two thousand pages away, she does attain it); the cattleya, the little phrase, Swann's error about Vinteuil, and so on and so on.

But it is my impression that for many many novels, almost all maybe, you could tell the plot in detachment from the details and have done with it. Whereas in a peculiar sense, which I should like somewhat to elucidate or winkle out of its shell, for Proust's novel, detail and plot are inseparable; and it is not too much to say that on every page one could find subject for comment that, to be really illuminating, would require comparisons throughout the novel.

I shall try to show something of all this by considering with you the relatively short chapter, "Place-Names: The Name," which follows after "Swann in Love" and concludes the first main division of the whole work, *Swann's Way*.

Its brevity itself is suggestive, for it is almost exactly the length of the "Overture" and therefore seems to suggest we look for symmetries and similarities of a deeper sort, of which we perceive immediately at least one—for it begins as the "Overture" did with a meditation on rooms, sleep, sleeplessness; and like that earlier meditation, it also is made up of a series of variations on the linked classes of images we have so often noticed. And it ends, too, with a meditation from many years later in the narrator's life (1913) quite strictly comparable with the passage near the end of the "Overture" where the narrator laments the deaths of his mother and father: "The wall of the staircase, up which I had watched the light of his candle gradually climb, was long ago demolished. And in myself, too, many things have perished. . . . "

But I observe already that if I get off on establishing the series of architectural correspondences I believe to exist, I shall wind up by having said scarcely anything of the chapter itself; I should perhaps not get past its first half dozen pages.

So I resolve to start again.

"Place-Names: The Name" is divided into three episodes. The first is a meditation on names, beginning with a memory of the narrator's room in the hotel at Balbec Plage, a place which, however, we do not reach in ordinary time for another two hundred pages; if indeed there is, in this strange book, any "ordinary time." The second is an account of the boy Marcel in earliest adolescence; he falls in love with Gilberte, and his love is connected with going out into society and the world, now exemplified in the mystery and glamor of the Swann family. The third episode, if so actionless a passage is an episode, is written and experienced many years after; it is the beautiful elegiac description of the Bois de Boulogne that I drew on, anticipating, in my last lecture.

Now that is reasonably efficient and accurate summary. It is a summary of what you presumably already know, for you have read the chapter too, but there is no great harm in that, and maybe it is the best part of the ritual reassurance afforded by the lecturer, that most of what he tells his hearers is what they already know; hearing confirmed what they already knew, they feel better—a little dull, maybe, but better.

But such summaries, though useful, even if much expanded and

filled in with detail, would not touch upon the essential difficulty—
which is also the essential charm—of Proust's way of composing,
so very different from what we are used to having from other
novelists. That way of composing may be related to my paradox: in
Proust, so little happens that we forget so much. The compositional
laws of this universe derive from a distortion imposed on time by
the putting together of chronological time with the utterly different
time of memory, as I observed earlier; and from what might be
symmetrically thought of as distortion of significance, or importance, so that very often great events go almost unremarked, while
little ones attract the most minute and scrupulous analysis. Swann's
marriage, for instance—would not most novelists have seen in that
a *scène à faire?* the crowning irony, to be rendered in the most
loving detail? Proust mentions it in passing. So too later on with
Swann's death, which we learn of as if by accident, in the mention
of "a visit of condolence" which a princess had paid to Mme. Swann
after the death of her husband—although that death had been
prepared and announced and elaborated on in the episode of the
duchess' red shoes two hundred pages before.

Consider for a contrast with what attention he describes the
telegram he sends Gilberte and the occasion of her first calling him
by his first name:

> Another time, being still obsessed by the desire to hear Berma in classic
> drama, I had asked her whether she had not a copy of a pamphlet in which
> Bergotte spoke of Racine, and which was now out of print. She had told me
> to let her know the exact title of it, and that evening I had sent her a little
> telegram, writing on its envelope the name, Gilberte Swann, which I had so
> often traced in my exercise-books. Next day she brought me in a parcel tied
> with pink bows and sealed with white wax, the pamphlet, a copy of which
> she had managed to find. "You see, it is what you asked me for," she said,
> taking from her muff the telegram that I had sent her. But in the address on
> the pneumatic message—which, only yesterday, was nothing, was merely a
> "little blue" that I had written, and, after a messenger had delivered it to
> Gilberte's porter and a servant had taken it to her in her room, had become
> a thing without value or distinction, one of the "little blues" that she had
> received in the course of the day—I had difficulty in recognising the futile,
> straggling lines of my own handwriting beneath the circles stamped on it at
> the post-office, the inscriptions added in pencil by a postman, signs of
> effectual realisation, seals of the external world, violet bands symbolical of

life itself, which for the first time came to espouse, to maintain, to raise, to rejoice my dream (I, 307).

> And there was another day on which she said to me: "You know, you may call me 'Gilberte'; in any case, I'm going to call you by your first name. It's too silly not to." Yet she continued for a while to address me by the more formal "*vous*," and, when I drew her attention to this, smiled, and composing, constructing a phrase like those that are put into the grammar-books of foreign languages with no other object than to teach us to make use of a new word, ended it with my Christian name. And when I recalled, later, what I had felt at the time, I could distinguish the impression of having been held, for a moment, in her mouth, myself, naked, without, any longer, any of the social qualifications which belonged equally to her other companions and, when she used my surname, to my parents, accessories of which her lips—by the effort that she made, a little after her father's manner, to articulate the words to which she wished to give a special value—had the air of stripping, of divesting me, as one peels the skin from a fruit of which one is going to put only the pulp into one's mouth, while her glance, adapting itself to the same new degree of intimacy as her speech, fell on me also more directly, not without testifying to the consciousness, the pleasure, even the gratitude that it felt, accompanying itself with a smile (I, 308).

The second example, since it bears on a name, may lead us to some further consideration of Proust's strange way of composing his book.

Names and Natures

For most readers, says de Maupassant, words have only a sense; what is necessary in addition is that they should have a soul. Here is Proust's way of thinking that thought:

> Words present to us little pictures of things, lucid and normal, like the pictures that are hung on the walls of schoolrooms to give children an illustration of what is meant by a carpenter's bench, a bird, an ant-hill; things chosen as typical of everything else of the same sort. But names present to us—of persons and of towns which they accustom us to regard as individual, as unique, like persons—a confused picture, which draws from the names, from the brightness or darkness of their sound, the colour in which it is uniformly painted, like one of those posters, entirely blue or entirely red, in which, on account of the limitations imposed by the process used in their reproduction, or by a whim on the designer's part, are blue or red not only the sky and the sea, but the ships and the church and the people in the streets (I, 296).

And in that first meditation of "Place-Names: The Name" he tells us a good many things both particular and of general import about the qualities of names and their impact upon early experience. For just as, when we are children, we learn first the words with which we shall later on say thoughtlessly, "I think" thus and such, so of many things in the world we receive first, with more or less sensitivity, their names, which are and perhaps for a long time remain all we know of their natures; and the same is true of people. In the novel, for example, it is the name of Swann, the name of Mme. Swann, which enshrine for the narrator his first vision of some almost divine mystery in society; it is at the putting together of the name Gilberte and the girl in the Champs Elysées that Marcel falls in love with her, and as we have seen, her taking of his name on her tongue is a kind of holy communion, as well as perhaps a kind of cannibalism (though curiously he does not give us readers the name itself, which is mentioned only twice in the book, and much later on, and given to Albertine). Also you will recollect with what great difficulty, on first seeing the Duchesse de Guermantes in church at Combray, he is able to associate this real woman with the great name that has taken his meditations back deep in time to the beginnings of France, and even further, to the emergence of those beginnings from mythology, from "the old-gold sonorous name of Brabant."

As it is with people, so with places. The following passage is an indicator of this great openness and suggestibility to the sounds of names that characterizes Marcel (and Proust):

> . . . Bayeux, so lofty in its noble coronet of rusty lace, whose highest point caught the light of the old gold of its second syllable; Vitré, whose acute accent barred its ancient glass with wooden lozenges; gentle Lamballe, whose whiteness ranged from egg-shell yellow to a pearly grey; Coutances, a Norman Cathedral, which its final consonants, rich and yellowing, crowned with a tower of butter; Lannion with the rumble and buzz, in the silence of its village street, of the fly on the wheel of the coach; Questambert, Pontorson, ridiculously silly and simple, white feathers and yellow beaks strewn along the road to those well-watered and poetic spots; Benodet, a name scarcely moored that seemed to be striving to draw the river down into the tangle of its sea-weeds; Pont-Aven, the snowy, rosy flight of the wing of a lightly poised coif, tremulously reflected in the greenish waters of a canal; Quimperlé,

more firmly attached, this, and since the Middle Ages, among the rivulets with which it balled, threading their pearls upon a grey background, like the pattern made, through the cobwebs upon a window, by rays of sunlight changed into blunt points of tarnished silver . . . (I, 297).

But, he tells us, "These images were false." First because they represent an accumulation of longing and association, not of fact; then because they are simplified, for "names themselves are not very comprehensive," and in the name for instance of Balbec, having only a few words from Legrandin and Swann to go on he is able to distinguish, "as in the magnifying glasses set in those penholders which one buys at seaside places," only "waves surging around a church built in the Persian manner." It is worth remarking a little more closely the sequence of illusion–disenchantment–revision or harmonizing of name and reality of which Marcel's experience of Balbec church is made up, for with respect to people as well as places it is probably the most characteristic architectural principle of the entire work.

Read Legrandin's and Swann's statements at I, 294:

"You feel, there, below your feet still," he had told me, "far more even than at Finistère (and even though hotels are now being superimposed upon it, without power, however, to modify that oldest bone in the earth's skeleton) you feel there that you are actually at the land's end of France, of Europe, of the Old World. And it is the ultimate encampment of the fishermen, precisely like the fishermen who have lived since the world's beginning, facing the everlasting kingdom of the sea-fogs and shadows of the night." One day when, at Combray, I had spoken of this coast, this Balbec, before M. Swann, hoping to learn from him whether it was the best point to select for seeing the most violent storms, he had replied: "I should think I did know Balbec! The church at Balbec, built in the twelfth and thirteenth centuries, and still half romanesque, is perhaps the most curious example to be found of our Norman gothic, and so exceptional that one is tempted to describe it as Persian in its inspiration."

Compare now I, 501–502, and its conclusion:

. . . as for Balbec, no sooner had I set foot in it than it was as though I had broken open a name which ought to have been kept hermetically closed, and into which . . . a tramway, a Cafe, people crossing the square, the local branch of a Bank, had come crowding into the interior of those two syllables which, closing over them, let them now serve as a border to the porch of the Persian church, and would never henceforward cease to contain them (I, 501–502).

For a good many novelists, one imagines, disillusionment with reality would have been the end of the experience, and to some extent as it were its moral. But with Proust there is always or at least very often a third phase. For much later in that first summer at Balbec he meets the painter Elstir, and is taught how romantic dream and reality may come into phase with one another if—and we suspect the young Marcel does not at this point take the lesson—if and only if we look with the eye of the artist.

> The effort made by Elstir to strip himself, when face to face with reality, of every intellectual concept, was all the more admirable in that this man who, before sitting down to paint, made himself deliberately ignorant, forgot, in his honesty of purpose, everything that he knew, since what one knows ceases to exist by itself, had in reality an exceptionally cultivated mind. When I confessed to him the disappointment that I had felt upon seeing the porch at Balbec: "What!" he had exclaimed, "you were disappointed by the porch! Why, it's the finest illustrated Bible that the people have ever had. That Virgin, and all the bas-reliefs telling the story of her life, they are the most loving, the most inspired expression of that endless poem of adoration and praise in which the middle ages extolled the glory of the Madonna. If you only knew, side by side with the most scrupulous accuracy in rendering the sacred text, what exquisite ideas the old carver had, what profound thoughts, what delicious poetry! . . .
>
> I told him also that I had gone there expecting to find an almost Persian building, and that this had doubtless been one of the chief factors in my disappointment. "Indeed, no," he assured me, "it is perfectly true. Some parts of it are quite oriental; one of the capitals reproduces so exactly a Persian subject that you cannot account for it by the persistence of Oriental traditions. The carver must have copied some casket brought from the East by explorers." And he did indeed shew me, later on, the photograph of a capital on which I saw dragons that were almost Chinese devouring one another, but at Balbec this little piece of carving had passed unnoticed by me in the general effect of the building which did not conform to the pattern traced in my mind by the words, "an almost Persian church" (I, 632–33).

So we may say that for Marcel's romanticizing, medievalizing mind, formed by names and images from history and painting and cathedral architecture as well as by images of the natural world, the name of a thing, a place, a person, is its soul, or logos. His coming into actual contact with the place or person deprives it as it were of its soul; it loses the powerful spirit enshrined in the name; only much later, and not always, a fresh act of imaginative sympathy, or true perception, may restore the spirit, though in a much altered form, to the object.

This observation may enable us to understand something more about the characteristic connections among the images in Proust. As his novel is a pedagogical novel having for subject matter the question How does one grow up? so there is an imitation, or analogy, of that question carried on in the images, perhaps especially in the persistent strain of images having to do with mechanical devices that in one way and another alter our perceptions: magic lantern, bioscope, binoculars, telescope, and many others, including the telephone. This analogous question asks about the growing up of the world itself, and especially about the great changes involved in the introduction of machine technology.

And I note in this connection that the authors who by common consent are the ones enshrined as masters in the modern canon covered in their life spans that most dramatic of changes, from the nineteenth to the twentieth century, from a world, however complex, of horse-drawn vehicles, trains, and letter-writing to a world of automobile, airplane, telephone, and telegraph. The abruptness with which the meditative and prophetic perception of the artist was altered may be seen most dramatically, perhaps, in the history of painting, from the impressionists and Cézanne through to the introduction, early in the new century, of cubism. And I note in passing that one complex phenomenon characterizes equally in different ways the solutions of Cézanne, cubists such as Picasso, Braque, Juan Gris, and pointillist variations of imagism such as in Seurat and Signac, and that is the spreading imposition of the city and its scientizing, geometrizing spirit upon nature. We may have occasion to consider this in more detail when we come to think about Proust's artist figure Elstir a bit later on. For the present it is enough to observe on this theme that Proust's mechanisms, quaint as they may appear to us now in the light of the past quarter-century, if it is a light, run all the way from that harmless producer of illusion, the magic lantern, to the first bombing raids, those prophetic annunciations of the new world being born.

Now the question of names and naming, and how names relate

to natures, requires a bit of placing of a historical kind in order that we may get a fuller view of why it is so important in Proust.

Until very recent times, certainly as late as the eighteenth century, it was the common view of civilized as of rude society that names represented magical essences, and were more real than the things they named. Not that this view had not been under debate for many centuries, or even since philosophizing began—Socrates considers it, amusingly but without getting much further than anyone else, in the *Cratylus*. And in the late Middle Ages the question came up in the controversy between nominalists and realists which some historians tell us was of decisive importance for the course of modern history and the possible doom of the human species; Egon Friedell, for instance, in his *Cultural History of the Modern Age*, regards the nominalist victory as more influential over history than the introduction of gunpowder or the invention of movable type (events roughly contemporary with it).

Now, whatever we believe about the nominalist or realist views of the matter, names remain for us entities of supreme importance even if they are ghosts. Persons who habitually speak of their own and the world's troubles as identity-crises and feelings of anomie and alienation will not dispute this proposition. The English writer Nigel Dennis, in a most entertaining essay prefaced to his *Two Plays*, says that if one examines critically all the possible bases for believing one is oneself one ends with that flimsiest-looking foundation of all, one's name—that breath of peculiarly shaped air—as the sole survivor. To give but one instance of the power conferred by names even in the modern world: if you know someone's name you can get his number and telephone him, thus compelling him at least to contemplate doing things he would not have been thinking of; and our innocent-sounding expression "call someone up" may indeed conceal in a metaphor the thought that in using the telephone we are evoking someone's spirit, for name and voice are equally identified in primitive thought with soul. Indeed, for a writer so sensitive as Proust, who is also faced with the telephone when its use is new and unexpected, the most relevant and revealing ideas come up when he uses the telephone for the first time, to phone his beloved grandmother from Doncières.

One morning, Saint-Loup confessed to me that he had written to my grandmother to give her news of me, with the suggestion that, since there was telephonic connexion between Paris and Doncières, she might make use of it to speak to me. In short, that very day she was to give me a call, and he advised me to be at the post office at about a quarter to four. . . . Like all of us nowadays I found not rapid enough for my liking in its abrupt changes the admirable sorcery for which a few moments are enough to bring before us, invisible but present, the person to whom we have been wishing to speak, and who, while still sitting at his table, in the town in which he lives (in my grandmother's case, Paris), under another sky than ours, in weather that is not necessarily the same, in the midst of circumstances and worries of which we know nothing, but of which he is going to inform us, finds himself suddenly transported hundreds of miles (he and all the surroundings in which he remains immured) within reach of our ear, at the precise moment which our fancy has ordained. And we are like the person in the fairy-tale to whom a sorceress, on his uttering the wish, makes appear with supernatural clearness his grandmother or his betrothed in the act of turning over a book, of shedding tears, of gathering flowers, quite close to the spectator and yet ever so remote, in the place in which she actually is at the moment. We need only, so that the miracle may be accomplished, apply our lips to the magic orifice and invoke—occasionally for rather longer than seems to us necessary, I admit—the Vigilant Virgins to whose voices we listen every day without ever coming to know their faces, and who are our Guardian Angels in the dizzy realm of darkness whose portals they so jealously keep; the All Powerful by whose intervention the absent rise up at our side, without our being permitted to set eyes on them; the Danaids of the Unseen who without ceasing empty, fill, transmit the urns of sound; the ironic Furies who, just as we were murmuring a confidence to a friend, in the hope that no one was listening, cry brutally: "I hear you!"; the ever infuriated servants of the Mystery, the umbrageous priestesses of the Invisible, the Young Ladies of the Telephone.

And, the moment our call has sounded, in the night filled with phantoms to which our ears alone are unsealed, a tiny sound, an abstract sound— the sound of distance overcome—and the voice of the dear one speaks to us (I, 809–10).

Observe, please, that when I spoke of "calling someone up" as of an evocation of the spirit, even of the dead, you thought of it as a joke, though not a very good one. But you are allowed so to regard it only out of habit, that sinister manager of our affairs, which in making you comfortable in your lives has also made you somewhat insensitive. Proust, however, sees the making of a phone call as a great mystery, which it is, and speaks of it in fitting terms of (slightly parodied) dread: it is sorcery, a miracle, magic; the operators are thought of as guardian angels, the voice of the beloved is "a real presence" which is, however, being disembodied, "a premonition of an eternal separation." And when he is cut off he feels he has lost "a beloved ghost," and reminds himself of Orpheus repeating the name of Eurydice. The incident ends, also, with one of Proust's ludicrous horrors: Marcel is paged, the call has been put through again: "Is that you, Granny?" and a woman with a strong English accent answers: "Yes, but I don't know your voice."

Returning to the identification of voice and name and soul or spirit or logos, here are some descriptions and examples drawn from the first chapter of Robert Briffault's wonderful book *The Mothers,* "In the Beginning Was the Word."

> That incorruptible essence of the species, of which particular individuals are, as it were, but participating aspects of emanations, is no other than the name of the species; for, in all primitive thought, the name of a person, or of a thing, is identical with the person or thing itself. A person's name is regarded as the substance of his breath, which he emits when he utters it, his spirit or soul. The word "soul" is from a Gothic root denoting wind; Greek psyche is derived from psycho, "to blow." The Semitic term for the creative name of the gods is the same as that for "breath" or "spirit." Similarly in most languages "name," "breath," "soul," are closely allied words which were, there can be little doubt, originally identical: Latin anima, nomen, Greek onoma, anemos, or in Celtic ainm (name), anim (soul), in Gothic anan, anadl.*

He follows on with many examples of primitive prohibitions concerning the use of names—including the marvelous instance of an Irish poet who quite failed to curse a certain king of Ulster "whose name would not scan in any known meter"—and identifies the magical power of names with the art of poetry: "the exalted title of poet, that is to say, 'maker' or 'creator,' was not originally bestowed upon composers of verse on account of special honour attaching to artistic and imaginative creation, but because 'poets' were originally magicians, wonder-workers, and were primarily in that sense 'creators' "†; that is to say, they were called "makers" not merely because they made things (the sense of the Greek *poiein*) but because the things they made made things happen: In the

---

*Robert Briffault, *The Mothers* (3 vols.; London, 1952), I, 8–9.
†*Ibid.,* 17.

beginning was the word, and it was not until Goethe's time that Faust revised it to read In the beginning was the deed.

Now I am fairly certain that Briffault's great study is not much in favor among ethnologists—though one such, seeing a volume of it on my desk, said, when he had got over his surprise, "You know, he's coming back." But if we read the very latest thing, which I take to be fairly represented by Claude Lévi-Strauss's *The Savage Mind*—a title which will take an emphasis on either word—we see that although much new information has changed much in theory the fact of the primitive emphasis on the importance of names in composing the world has if anything been overwhelmingly confirmed. In a chapter of that book which, without mentioning Proust, is nevertheless called "Time Regained," Lévi-Strauss says a couple of things that seem to make the relation I am trying to expound. He speaks of savage thought as "definable both by a consuming symbolic ambition such as humanity has never again seen rivalled, and by scrupulous attention directed entirely towards the concrete, and finally by the implicit conviction that these two attitudes are one." This in itself suggests to me the style and compositional method of Proust, and that power his work has, which I have tried to describe to you, of being compresent everywhere with itself, of being entirely contained in the instance as the oak in the acorn, of being the vast systematic exfoliating of a single thought till it becomes the world. A page before, Lévi-Strauss remarks in passing: "There are still zones in which savage thought, like savage species, is relatively protected. This is the case of art, to which our civilisation accords the status of a national park, with all the advantages and inconveniences attending so artificial a formula; and it is particularly the case of so many as yet 'uncleared' sectors of social life, where, through indifference or inability, and most often without our knowing why, primitive thought continues to flourish."*

The foregoing brief excursion into other realms may enable us to see some things about art and imagination most often hidden from view. The comparison of the artist and the primitive is well

*Claude Lévi-Stauss, *The Savage Mind* (Chicago, 1967), 219.

known; a little or a lot too well known. For now, in the researches of modern ethnologists the primitive turns out to be not primitive at all, in the sense, somewhat prideful, pejorative, or contemptuous, in which the term still continues to be used; that is, primitive societies make articulations of the universe not simpler and more inadequate than ours, but, on the contrary, vastly more comprehensive and systematized and vastly more detailed, as well as vastly fuller of observation, than our own.* It may be that the artist, to the extent that he is like a primitive, is so because he too is moved by "a consuming symbolic ambition such as humanity has never again seen rivalled, and by scrupulous attention directed entirely toward the concrete, and finally by the implicit conviction that these two attitudes are one."

We need not, perhaps, go the length of envisioning Marcel Proust as a field anthropologist working the rich tribal lore of the Faubourg St.-Germain and of French middle-class society. Yet it is clear not only that names are of the first importance for the young Marcel, but that another sector of the book, the part dealing with the aristocracy, preoccupies itself richly with the matter of names and titles, as well as with the magical question of who it is that inhabits name and title.

*Than, I mean, what any one of us should be able to make of the landscape around us in terms of numbers of species, edibility, and other usefulness. The sciences, taking this as meaning all of the learnings, all the knowledges, have built up, of course, structures vaster and more complex—so much so, indeed, that none of us can any longer know enough, of his own knowledge, to come in out of the rain.

VIII

One of you has proposed to me the subject of exaggeration, parody, caricature, in Proust's drawing of his characters, and today I hope to put before you some reflections on this fascinating and rather teasing theme. Probably I shall finish by saying: Proust's novel does not confine itself to realism; but then neither does the world. For before we can decide whether Proust exaggerates the traits of his people, or whether his doing so is a fault or a virtue, we shall have to unpack our own notions of what character is, and spread these out visibly, in order to see if we understand what we ourselves assume we mean.

Here are three statements from Valéry's essay on Proust which seem to me thematic and of great interest for our question.

1. "The group which calls itself society is composed only of symbolic figures. Each of its members represents some abstraction."

2. "Just as a banknote is only a slip of paper, so the member of Society is a sort of fiduciary money made of living flesh."

3. Great art "is the art of simplified figures and the most pure types; of essences which permit the symmetrical and almost musical development of the consequences arising from a carefully isolated situation."

In a recent lecture my colleague J. V. Cunningham has put the matter with epigrammatic clarity and decisiveness. His subject is

"Ideal Fiction," his example "The Clerk's Tale," and it is a pleasure to quote almost all of his concluding paragraphs.

> In ideal fiction the characters are flat. But it is a fiction of our fiction that people are really round. The truth is we are not usually real life characters in real life. We are flat, and so are those we know. We are only round occasionally to others in a sympathetic moment, to ourselves in introspection, and now and again as a demand on others in the grim game of interpersonal relations: "I want to be treated as a person." We usually see others as truck drivers or neighbors, bore or blonde. And we are flat to ourselves when working efficiently, when we are most ourselves. When I write a poem I am a poet; I am narrowed to relevance.
>
> Nor was the extreme case in Chaucer's world as extreme as one might think. In that Christianity that has been almost liquidated in my lifetime, each of us is an extreme case, destined for heaven or for hell. There is no individualistic limbo in which we as real characters can hide. We are flat, flatly saved or flatly damned. The ultimate world is ideal, and the ultimate our ultimate concern.

As you probably are aware, the terms *flat character* and *round character* were introduced into discussions of fiction by E. M. Forster in his handbook *Aspects of the Novel,* where the distinction amounted almost if not quite to that between minor characters and major characters, comic characters and heroic ones. It was a distinction by which I imagine many people, including myself, were impressed; and now Professor Cunningham has disposed of it, I think correctly, illustrating a principle enunciated by Scott Fitzgerald: the opposite of any widely held opinion is usually worth a small fortune to someone; and illustrating, more valuably, how when we take unto ourselves received opinions, on whatever authority, we merely prevent ourselves from thinking.

Now the word *character,* which began in Greek and continued in Latin as meaning first either an engraved or scratched mark or else the tool for making such a mark, presently got the transferred literary sense of *style* (for *stylus* was the tool with which you scratched the letters of the alphabet, also called *characters*). So it is from the start a very literary word, a writer's word, and only much later gets transferred over to the persons depicted by writing. The OED says that the word first appears, in its modern, novelistic sense, in Fielding's *Tom Jones,* in 1749.

From its physical and instrumental origin the word seems to retain something of narrowness, of simplification; and indeed *character* in a work of fiction almost always means moral character and character in relation to the action: it might be defined as the handful of traits supplied to a person by the author which make it plausible for that person to do what he does, that is, what the story must have him do. Oedipus, for example, is supplied by Sophocles with a couple of traits—stubbornness, haste, extreme irritability—not because a historical Oedipus had these traits but because the story (in this sense the term *story* is equivalent to Oedipus's *fate*) requires him to be a man that does rash things and persists in doing them over all advice and warning. So it is plausible for Oedipus to fall and suffer as he does, but divine necessity, the oracle (and its equivalent, the action Sophocles adapted for his play) make it necessary for Oedipus to suffer as he does, quite apart from any question of his character.

Now Proust's novel is ever so much more complex than Sophocles' play, and there are many more characters: an index made by the editors of the Pléiade edition lists all the major appearances of every name of every person in the book, and occupies all by itself over a hundred pages. And yet for all this complexity it may be that the principle is not affected: character is the handful of traits supplied to a person by the author which make it plausible for that person to do what he does, that is, what the story must have him do.

But ever so many people in Proust don't, in the conventional novelist's sense, *do anything.* They appear for a moment only, under the form of an anecdote, and vanish: like Swann's father, or like the wonderful lady who whenever she goes out in society and is bidden by her hostess to a chair sees a man already sitting in it, and has all her life to decide which is the hallucination, the hostess' gesture or the man in the chair. Such people *are* anecdotes. And it is very often by the means of anecdote that Proust makes his foreground characters emerge as well; by anecdote, and by a degree of comic exaggeration along a scale running from plain extravagance—as with the hotel manager at Balbec, characterized by malapropisms that he commits at the rate of at least one per sentence over a couple of pages—to a subtlety that will fill us with doubts as to our own view of what is real, for in the novelistic equation you have not simply the character observed and depicted *as he is*; no, you have always, and of greatest import, the eye that observes and the mind that depicts, its metaphors and divagations. About this I observe once again that the mind in Proust is double, it contains at the same time and not always distinguishably the experience of the young Marcel and the knowledge of the old narrator; under cover of the latter, too, it slips in as knowledge a good many things belonging necessarily to imaginative inference, such as for example the analyses of the state of mind of persons who never say anything about their state of mind.

Now I want to look closely into Proust's presentation of a major character and hope to show something of how this doubleness works to give as it were depth to our experience of the persons and their world. And I hope to do this not so much as a reader under the spell of the illusion, but rather as a critic who is wondering about the means and the meaning of the illusion.

The Baron de Charlus is a pivotal character in the book; he is much and he represents much, so that his Luciferian pride, his Luciferian disgrace and fall, are the pride and fall of a great aristocracy. I suppose his reputation has spread sufficiently beyond the confines of the novel that it comes as no surprise to you, even if you are on your first reading, that he is a homosexual. But it does come as a surprise to Marcel the young man, who is in some respects perhaps exceedingly naive, and does not even think of this explanation of the presented facts until about halfway through the novel, when he sees it with the seeing of the eye; whereupon much that had puzzled him about the Baron becomes clear. So that the introduction of the Baron to Marcel and to the world of the novel is as it were an exercise in Proustian vision, comparable in some ways with the problem of vision in Elstir's paintings, where what the eye sees does not at first harmonize with what the mind thinks it knows, so that the mind helplessly and more or less vainly formulates hypotheses to explain the facts as they appear.

Before the Baron makes his first appearance in person he has been a rumored presence. At Combray, where Marcel saw him once, he was said to be Mme. Swann's lover, but we learn that according to Swann and Saint-Loup this simply could not be true, though we are not told why. On the other hand, Swann suspects the Baron among others of having possibly written him the anonymous letter about Odette.

His entrance at Balbec is preluded by some things Saint-Loup says about him; his first name, Palamède, sets off a characteristic sequence of images;

> . . . Palamède, a name that had come down to him from his ancestors, the Princes of Sicily. And later on when I found, as I read history, belonging to this or that Podesta or Prince of the Church, the same Christian name, a fine renaissance medal—some said, a genuine antique—that had always remained in the family, having passed from generation to generation, from the Vatican cabinet to the uncle of my friend, I felt the pleasure that is reserved for those who, unable from lack of means to start a case of medals, or a picture gallery, look out for old names (names of localities, instructive and picturesque as an old map, a bird's-eye view, a sign-board or a return of customs; baptismal names, in which rings out and is plainly heard, in their fine French endings, the defect of speech, the intonation of a racial vulgarity, the vicious pronunciation by which our ancestors made Latin and Saxon words undergo lasting mutilations which in due course became the august law-givers of our grammar books) and, in short, by drawing upon their collections of ancient and sonorous words, give themselves concerts like the people who acquire viols da gamba and viols d'amour so as to perform the music of days gone by upon old-fashioned instruments (I, 566–67).

His pride, remarkable even in a society based on pride, is commented on; and Saint-Loup tells an anecdote about Charlus and two friends beating up a homosexual:

> "One day, a man who just now is very much in the eye, as Balzac would say, of the Faubourg Saint-Germain, but who at a rather awkward period of his early life displayed odd tastes, asked my uncle to let him come to this place. But no sooner had he arrived than it was not to the ladies but to my uncle Palamède that he began to make overtures. My uncle pretended not to understand, made an excuse to send for his two friends; they appeared on the scene, seized the offender, stripped him, thrashed him till he bled, and then with twenty degrees of frost outside kicked him into the street where he was found more dead than alive; so much so that the police started an inquiry which the poor devil had the greatest difficulty in getting them to abandon. My uncle would never go in for such drastic methods now, in fact you can't conceive the number of men of humble position that he, who is so haughty

with people in society, has shewn his affection, taken under his wing, even if he is paid for it with ingratitude" (I, 567).

This little story functions in a number of ways, for when Charlus is introduced a page later it accounts for Marcel's not pitching on inversion for the explanation of his behavior, even while it introduces musically as it were the themes of insolence, superbia, shocking violence, the police, and, as a contrast, the innocent affection Charlus is said to show for young men. So it arouses our suspicions while preventing Marcel from having any.

Charlus, when Marcel at last sees him next morning, is described chiefly with respect to his eyes and the way he uses them, which evoke in the young man's mind a series of alarmed and alarming hypotheses (I, 568ff), of which I shall excerpt some of the most significant.

His eyes were "dilated with observation"; "every now and then those eyes were shot through by a look of intense activity such as the sight of a person whom they do not know excites only in men to whom . . . it suggests thoughts that would not occur to anyone else—madmen, for instance, or spies." The look he flashes at Marcel suggests a last shot fired at an enemy before one turns to flee. He seems to be on stage, making a couple of gestures that people make when they mean to show their annoyance at being kept waiting, "although they never make it when they are really waiting," and breathing hard as people do "who are not feeling too hot but would like it to be thought that they were." Marcel suspects him of being a hotel crook planning to rob his grandmother and himself, and hesitates between thinking of him as a thief and as a lunatic. He glances at Marcel again, and the glance suggests "the steeped look that we see on the faces of certain hypocrites, the smug look on those of certain fools." A few moments after he is compared to a detective on special duty, and some pages later we have this: "his eyes, which were never fixed on the person to whom he was speaking, strayed perpetually in all directions, like those of certain animals when they are frightened, or those of street hawkers who, while they are bawling out their patter and displaying their illicit merchandise, keep a sharp look-out" for the police (I, 574).

But now, having been introduced by Mme. de Villeparisis,
Marcel can no longer entertain the supposition that the Baron is a
crook or a detective or a madman, and has to consider the revelation
of those eyes, that stare, as the revelation of "some incognito, some
disguise assumed by a powerful man in danger, or merely by a
dangerous—but tragic—person" (I, 575).

Mingled with these descriptions of Charlus in terms of eye and
glance are allusions to his clothing, respectable and even distinguished yet also a trifle mystifying:

> . . . when one came near him one felt that if colour was almost entirely absent
> from these garments it was not because he who had banished it from them
> was indifferent to it but rather because for some reason he forbade himself
> the enjoyment of it. And the sobriety which they displayed seemed to be of
> the kind that comes from obedience to a rule of diet rather than from want
> of appetite. A dark green thread harmonised, in the stuff of his trousers, with
> the clock on his socks, with a refinement which betrayed the vivacity of a
> taste that was everywhere else conquered, to which this single concession had
> been made out of tolerance for such a weakness, while a spot of red on his
> necktie was imperceptible, like a liberty which one dares not take (I, 570).

> At that moment, noticing that the embroidered handkerchief which he
> had in his pocket was shewing some coloured threads, he thrust it sharply
> down out of sight with the scandalised air of a prudish but far from innocent
> lady concealing attractions which, by an excess of scrupulosity, she regards
> as indecent (I, 578).

and to his voice which, when he uttered certain delicate sentiments,

> . . . took on an unexpected sweetness and seemed to be embodying choirs of
> betrothed maidens, of sisters, who poured out the treasures of their love. But
> the bevy of young girls, whom M. de Charlus in his horror of every kind of
> effeminacy would have been so distressed to learn that he gave the impression
> of sheltering thus within his voice, did not confine themselves to the inter-
> pretation, the modulation, of scraps of sentiment. Often while M. de Charlus
> was talking one could hear their laughter, shrill, fresh laughter of school-
> girls or coquettes quizzing their partners with all the archness of clever
> tongues and pretty wits (I, 577).

To clinch the matter, Marcel's grandmother, even while
delighted with Charlus for his higher qualities and for his knowledge of Mme. de Sévigné's Letters (I, 572, 576), finds in him, with
the clear accuracy of observation that comes from disinterested

goodness "a delicacy, a sensibility that were quite feminine" (I, 576).

I have quoted at considerable length in order that we may have an illustration before us to make some observations about. I imagine you will agree that a good deal of comic exaggeration and parody is going on in the depiction of M. de Charlus, though I may have heightened that impression by putting together the most salient hits. And yet there is a pretty problem having to do with exagger ation, that you may not, as readers of fiction, ever have considered. As a problem of artistic representation generally, it may be expressed thus: confronted with a book or a painting, we can never have access to the reality it is said to represent, hence we can never judge by that means, of direct comparison, the degree of its truth.

Observe that even photography, which can give us, say, a replica of Cézanne's favorite hillside, does not change this situation, for it cannot give us the hillside refracted through Cézanne's genius, his training, his brushwork, his materials, and his tradition. The photograph gives us what is called a fact—as though light and its variations were not also facts.

With writers, I go on to observe, exaggeration *is* truth. Just as the gestures of actors, before electric light and movies, had to be operatically large and exaggerated simply in order to be visible to the audience, so the writer takes from the welter of sense impressions and imaginative inferences the few items he regards as significant, for whatever reason, and draws these with great boldness, in order that we, with no object before us but the printed page, may be possessed by the illusion of a reality behind it.

How then should we judge of the fidelity to life of an artistic representation? and does it matter? Concerning this, someone once said: a literary critic, having learned from much reading what life is like, spends his professional life berating authors because their books are not like real life.

Of course they are not; nor is a telescope like a star or a stethoscope like a heartbeat or a piano like a sonata. Reverting to one of those sayings of Valéry, "Great art is the art of simplified figures and of the most pure types; of essences which permit the symmetrical and almost musical development of the consequences arising from a carefully isolated situation."

If you will consider again the introduction of M. de Charlus in the light of this claim, I think you will see that it is not fidelity to appearance that counts, that is the value of artistic composition, but, far rather, the intensity and serenity of vision that can compass so much and work in several ways at once. This is another of Proust's ways of showing the oak in the acorn. For although young Marcel has not hit on the one explanation that would fit together and resolve in a single motion the traits displayed by the Baron, neither is he wrong in the comparisons he resorts to, which musically prophesy a large part of the action of the novel: as inversion is the secret center that relates the aristocracy to the proletariat and the underworld, so M. de Charlus and the world he increasingly comes to inhabit are characterized by what Marcel sees in his eyes at their first meeting: madness, criminality, violence, spying, detectives, thieves. All these ideas, which enter thus as hypotheses, do presently become realities in the action. At the same time, the grandmother is not wrong in being charmed by M. de Charlus' better qualities, which he has, though intermittently, in some abundance. And this progression is also characteristically Proustian: we are at first mistaken about someone; but our mistake was never quite altogether that; so far as it was based on keen observation and equally keen endeavor to imagine, that is, to formulate a law or hypothesis that will account for the observation, the mistake will turn out to be true after all, but in an unexpected way.

We may proceed with some rather more general reflections. An imaginative fiction, and this one especially, for reasons I have given you several times, is a peculiar compound of inward and outward, of observation and imagination, or dream. The characters in it, we shall do well to remember, exist for the author and thence they exist for us; they do not exist on their own. Moreover, the author is all the characters, though some of them only momentarily, and thence by his art we are all the characters, though in a less immediate way.

Though a remark like that is susceptible of a mystical and anagogic reading, I mean it in the first place for a matter of fact, and simply demonstrable. Proust's biographer George Painter warns his readers very early on against attempting to identify the originals of the characters; yet as he proceeds in his study he casually disregards his own warning, speaking of Charles Haas as the original of Swann, of Anatole France as the original of Bergotte, even once referring to Claude Monet as "Elstir himself!" Charlus, Painter's index tells me, is a composite of traits drawn from five real people, among them Comte Robert de Montesquiou, an author whose style Proust is said to parody in the style of Charlus' speeches. But in his text Painter makes it abundantly clear that in addition to the five people, Proust himself is a source for Charlus. Nor does he mean simply by appearance or characteristic; no, he means that things that happened to certain persons in real life were applied in the novel to Charlus, and that certain anecdotes from the very darkest part of the author's life were transferred by him to Charlus in the novel. So that one can see how the art work depends in part upon observation and memory, yes, but depends even more upon the artist's power of freely combining and recombining the elements supplied by observation and memory so that the combination will serve his own necessity and that of his book.

In speaking of the author's own necessity as possibly separate from that of his book I also mean something I hope is quite simple. Zeus was known to the Greeks as all-powerful, but there was one thing more powerful than he, and that was fatal necessity. So with the author, who is the creator deity of his book and its people, but yet is himself subordinate to the laws which the book develops as it goes along. Yet while he is subject to those laws the author is nevertheless working out as it were his own destiny in that of his world and its people; his book will be, when it is rounded out, a Day of Judgment in which he is both God and sinner. So that the work of the artist is in one sense a disguised confession, in which aspects of himself are isolated and given the appearance of persons living in the world; and such a figure as that of Charlus may have meant for Proust confession, atonement, penance, and ritual of riddance all at once, a way of representing the horrors of his own nature on the grandest possible scale—that Charlus is Lucifer is made plain by, among other things, his references to archangels as

his special patrons and protectors—and subject to the most pre-
cipitous fall and punishment, with the purgative or even redemptive
conclusion, however, that in the course of his descent into Sodom
and old age and illness the Baron is last seen in harmless senility,
all the viciousness and pride drained from him as, mothered by
Jupien his former lover and pimp, he says over *"avec un dureté
presque triomphale"* the list of the names of the dead: "Hannibal de
Bréauté, mort! Antoine de Mouchy, mort! Charles Swann, mort!
Adalbert de Montmorency, mort! Boson de Talleyrand, mort!
Sosthène de Doudeauville, mort!" (P, III, 862; translation, II, 989).
And each time, says the narrator, that word *dead* seemed to fall on
the defunct like a heavier clod of earth thrown by a gravedigger
with intent to dig them deeper in the tomb.

A friend recently said to me: "How can you like Proust so
much when you know he was such an awful little man?" I said:
"Because if he could work through his awfulness maybe there's
some hope for the rest of us." In a subsequent lecture focused on
art and the artist in Proust's novel, I shall try to say something of
that hope.

IX

Examples for Proust's comedy: introduction to two royal personages.

a. Princesse de Luxembourg, I, 530

b. Princesse de Parme, I, 1023–24

Proust rarely writes scenes. Like Wagner, he is continuous:

The other musician, he who was delighting me at this moment, Wagner, retrieving some exquisite scrap from a drawer of his writing-table to make it appear as a theme, retrospectively necessary, in a work of which he had not been thinking at the moment when he composed it, then having composed a first mythological opera, and a second, and afterwards others still, and perceiving all of a sudden that he had written a tetralogy, must have felt something of the same exhilaration as Balzac, when, casting over his words the eye at once of a stranger and of a father, finding in one the purity of Raphael, in another the simplicity of the Gospel, he suddenly decided, as he shed a retrospective illumination upon them, that they would be better brought together in a cycle in which the same characters would reappear, and added to his work, in this act of joining it together, a stroke of the brush, the last and the most sublime. A unity that was ulterior, not artificial, otherwise it would have crumbled into dust like all the other systematisations of mediocre writers who with the elaborate assistance of titles and sub-titles give themselves the appearance of having pursued a single and transcendent design. Not fictitious, perhaps indeed all the more real for being ulterior, for being born of a moment of enthusiasm when it is discovered to exist among fragments which need only to be joined together. A unity that has been unaware of itself, therefore vital and not logical, that has not banned variety, chilled execution. It emerges (only applying itself this time to the work as a whole) like a fragment composed separately, born of an inspiration, not

> required by the artificial development of a theme, which comes in to form an
> integral part of the rest (II, 490–491).

Even in such direct confrontations as that of Marcel with Charlus over the hat, nothing in the standard novelistic sense is "accomplished."

In return for this deferring of conclusions he gets the power of keeping many things going at once. In some way, this must be why the episodes are so hard to remember in order—because (a) almost nothing happens, even while (b) so much is happening at once. In exchange, however, the novel becomes its own memory, its own history, its own archaeology; a cumulative effect, that after a long time allows the most touching moments to be produced by an allusion to its own past, as for example at II, 518, where Marcel says to Brichot that he hoped by going to the Verdurins to see the room where Swann used to meet Odette, and Brichot replies: "so you know that old story, do you?" and adds "and yet from those days to the death of Swann is what the poet rightly calls *grande spatium mortalis aevi.*"

My illustration for Proust's narrative style—I might have chosen many another—is the episode of Marcel's first visit to the theater (I, 342–46).

Proust's (and Moncrieff's) style. Parody. The Proustian comedy and style of narrating.

No doubt very much perishes, and more suffers distortion, in a translation. Nevertheless, the translation we are reading has very distinct traits of its own, a sort of magic lantern replication of its original. And if I asked you, for a midterm exam, or a parody of a midterm exam, to parody a little scene from Shakespeare as Proust, through the lens of Scott Moncrieff, might have done it, that was owing to a conviction that in learning one must not always do things abstractly, in categories, and from without, but sometimes as a kind of imitative dance. I hope, and rather doubt, that many of you found the exercise pleasurable; that is in part because you have not been brought up to doing such things; nonetheless, I hope with more confidence that you found it somewhat instructive.

As I have suggested, there are two ways of doing this kind of thing, and they parallel two sorts of understanding. In one sort of understanding, you paraphrase what you read into other, usually much more abstract, language; in effect, you summarize it for convenience: as were you to "understand" the first paragraph of Proust by saying "It tells about someone in between sleep and waking." You would be correct, but not more than that. Similarly, you could write a parody of Proust by analytic methods, saying to yourself: I must use long sentences, I must get in a sequence of images that include names, colors, old cathedrals, disguises, a train or two, and an optical instrument, say a lorgnette. Again you would be correct, but not much more than that.

There is a second sort of understanding, and a second way of imitating, more mysterious and more immediate than the first; it amounts to a kind of dance, a bodily recognition of how things are, a current that connects you at once with the experience of the author's style. It is the sort of understanding that is most like seeing: there is no conscious interposing of abstract terms for understanding, there is no "analysis" or "explication," you just "see." My favorite example: you walk along the seashore, you pick up one stone out of a million stones; it attracts you, why? Because, you presently remember, Morris Graves by his paintings has taught you to recognize and to single out a certain range of textures that now become an identifiable part of the creation for you. But now I think of a better because more pertinent example. I once knew a man who very much resembled the Baron de Charlus. In fact, I was so struck with the resemblance that I thought of him, on our first becoming acquainted, as "the very type" of Charlus.

No doubt, looking back, I am able to list the resemblances: the man I am thinking of is tall but portly, even stout, and with a certain indolent arrogance of carriage and extravagance of gesture; is homosexual; is proud and capable of extreme rudeness and fits of violent ill temper; but is also genuinely tenderhearted and kindly; and so on. But I didn't begin with anything like that analysis; I began by thinking that here, by a species of literary pastiche nature probably indulges in oftener than we know, was M. de Charlus. I was not even reading Proust at that time.

And there is equally no doubt that were I to carry out my comparison by detailed reference to the text I should find that I was as much wrong as right; even that I had by degrees altered details of my acquaintance's appearance, his dress, his behavior, to make the comparison work better.

This is a teasing subject, and might take us in a number of directions at once. Many things this reading of Proust has led me to observe have forced me to see that our reading of the so-called real world is incurably literary. Nothing is ever, as people say—and how often they say it!—*objective*, for it always comes inseparably from a language and a style. For the present, though, I shall add only this, that the man of whom I am speaking is a man of considerable culture and has, of course, read Proust.

The parallel in parody or pastiche is this: you don't analyze the author's style so much as you become infected with it. This is an interesting though rather perilous procedure. It is also, if it is a poison, its own antidote, as Proust himself tells us:

> Let me say that the best advice I can give to my fellow writers is that they would be well advised to indulge in the cleansing, exorcising pastime of parody. When we come to the end of a book, we find that not only do we want to go on living with its characters . . . but that our own inner voice, which has grown accustomed, through the long hours of perusal, to follow the Balzacian or Flaubertian rhythm, insists on talking just like those authors. The one means of escape from the toil lies in letting the influence have its way for a while, in keeping one's foot on the pedal and permitting the resonance to continue: in other words, in embarking on a deliberate act of parody, with the object, once we have got the stuff out of our system, of becoming ourselves again instead of spending the rest of our working lives producing *unconscious* parodies.*

Observe how this description plays down the element of conscious analysis and description—which nevertheless Proust elsewhere does not slight; he can spend a page on Flaubert's use of the word *and*, while Marcel's descriptions of various literary styles to Albertine are full of the most refined observation—in favor of

---

*From *Pleasures and Days*, but I am quoting from Dwight MacDonald, *Parodies* (New York, 1960), pp. 501–502. See also Painter, *Proust: The Later Years* (Boston, 1965), II, 99–100.

something more passive: "letting the influence have its way . . .
permitting the resonance to continue."

It is not my subject today to inquire how this happens, this
marvelous silent understanding of a matter that is like perception,
or memory, more than it is like thinking. Yeats calls it the non-
chalance of the hand; Plato calls it "unspeakable" and Aristotle for
once agrees, it is "without word." But for the present I shall say
only that it is one of the truly great subjects, perhaps the greatest
of all, and I find it ever increasingly strange that colleges and
universities pay it as little heed as possible, that is to say, none.

As a prelude to my real subject for today, Proustian narration and
Proustian comedy, I shall impose upon your indulgence my own
midterm exam, a bit of *King Lear*, Proustified & Moncrieffed.

GLOUCESTER. No further, sir; a man may rot even here.
EDGAR.   What, in ill thoughts again? Men must endure
            Their going hence, even as their coming hither;
            Ripeness is all. Come on.
GLOUCESTER.   And that's true too.
Exeunt.

from *King Lear*, Act V, Scene ii.

That "ripeness is all" was a sentiment of which Edgar even now scarcely
believed the truth, and which, until a few days before, his character, formed
but secreted, as in the rough milkweed pod the seeds lie like the plated and
lapped armor of some hero of antiquity said by peasants to be not dead but
asleep and awaiting a resurrection, would not have permitted him to utter.
It may indeed have been that this not particularly distinguished young man
(for good breeding and ancient lineage do not necessarily provide their
possessors with those other qualities of mind and heart which age and much
experience of the world may possibly come to consider valuable) had attained
all at once to the making of this epigram more or less by chance, a means no
doubt despised by persons in society but not—for he knows too well how
many of the most sublime effects, strokes of wit such as, for example, the
small hole in the cloud portrayed by Tintoretto in his Ascension of Elijah in
the Palazzo Mocenigo, which is a real hole in the canvas, are reached rather
by luck than judgment—by the artist. So Edgar was able, but only after
having delivered himself of his remark, to perceive at once something of its
strangeness and truth, qualities to which, so long as he was no more than the
elegant sprig of nobility who had seen, in the spectacle of the three Lear girls,

Goneril, Regan, and Cordelia, no more than a single organism proliferating in an anonymous ambience of gold hair and flashing smiles, he could have been at best indifferent. We are taught by sufferings, in this world, and, as when the members of a charitable committee decide to subscribe a certain sum to a hospital, not pausing to reflect that one of them may lately have been ruined by an unfortunate speculation, no one asks whether we can afford the lessons. So that perhaps the profundity of Edgar's remark depended, after all, upon a very simple circumstance: that the sight of his father the aged Duke, in the blind helplessness of the very old so like that of earliest childhood, his now useless binoculars swinging at his side as, in an allegorical painting of the Middle Ages, saints are depicted as holding the instruments of their martyrdom, Lawrence his gridiron, Catharine her wheel, appealed to the son as holding something of that wealth of irony and strangeness which we feel even through our anger when, for example, our mistress, having pleaded indisposition when we know quite well—but do not dare to say— that she attended the opera in the company of the Duke of Cornwall, gains, in our eyes, something of the character of fatal necessity itself. So true is it that the profundities of our moral nature occur, for the most part, by accident, of which we may or may not realize entirely the mathematical implications before being overtaken by the last accident, death. It is also the effect of our perpetual masqueradings and disguisings, effect of which Edgar more than most had in the past days been made to feel the force, to induce in us wavering uncertainties, unstable though golden as the reflexion of sun on running water, concerning the reality, not merely of other people (which we continually suspect without being able finally to disprove) but of ourselves also, and even of life and the world itself; so that Edgar, not absolutely assured as to what degree, in playing the fool over so prolonged a period, he had been in fact a fool, or whether, as his grandmother so long ago told him it might, the momentary grimace had so frozen as to become the habitual expression of his face, felt in his own words, without at this time or for long after being able to solve the riddle of their meaning, a flickering illumination, fluid and dark as are said to be the waters of Acheron or Styx, lighted by the fires of hell, upon his own character. As he dragged from the field the old lord, whose infirmities gave him something of the appearance of a drunken person who has disgraced himself at a house to which he will never again be permitted to go, he reflected that the Duke, who had always been remarkable rather for the greatness of his name and the depth to which it could be traced in tradition than for any particular power of intellect or, indeed, perception, would very probably reply by some trivial but fashionable phrase indicative simultaneously of boredom and agreement, such as "very likely," or "that's true," and Edgar's satisfaction at having more or less exactly anticipated this rejoinder when it at last came, for the moment quite obscured his sense of the larger disaster to which they were a party. So it is, however, with each one of us; the momentary sense of superiority inspired in us by our own wit, however slight, makes bearable (though not, it is true, palatable) the most tragic defeat, by the same process of reasoning as that which makes the bankrupt, giving a dinner at which he plans to announce to his creditors the misfortunes and reverses whose effect he is about to transfer to them, take care that the food, the furnishings, the service, should be particularly exquisite on this occasion in the course of which he hopes somewhat to mitigate the shame of his failure by what will perhaps pass among people of fashion as a courageous wit.

As a convenient transition from this subject of parody to that of narrative style and comedy in Proust, here is, with Marcel's very funny and puzzled reflections on it, Albertine's imitation of Marcel:

She said to me (and I was, in spite of everything, deeply touched, for I thought to myself: Certainly I would not speak as she does, and yet, all the same, but for me she would not be speaking like this, she has come profoundly under my influence, she cannot therefore help loving me, she is my handiwork): "What I like about these foodstuffs that are cried is that a thing which we hear like a rhapsody changes its nature when it comes to our table and addresses itself to my palate. As for ices (for I hope that you won't order me one that isn't cast in one of those old-fashioned moulds which have every architectural shape imaginable), whenever I take one, temples, churches, obelisks, rocks, it is like an illustrated geography-book which I look at first of all and then convert its raspberry or vanilla monuments into coolness in my throat." I thought that this was a little too well expressed, but she felt that I thought that it was well expressed, and went on, pausing for a moment when she had brought off her comparison to laugh that beautiful laugh of hers which was so painful to me because it was so voluptuous. "Oh dear, at the Ritz I'm afraid you'll find Vendôme Columns of ice, chocolate ice or raspberry, and then you will need a lot of them so that they may look like votive pillars or pylons erected along an avenue to the glory of Coolness. They make raspberry obelisks too, which will rise up here and there in the burning desert of my thirst, and I shall make their pink granite crumble and melt deep down in my throat which they will refresh better than any oasis" (and here the deep laugh broke out, whether from satisfaction at talking so well, or in derision of herself for using such hackneyed images, or, alas, from a physical pleasure at feeling inside herself something so good, so cool, which was tantamount to a sensual satisfaction). "Those mountains of ice at the Ritz sometimes suggest Monte Rosa, and indeed, if it is a lemon ice, I do not object to its not having a monumental shape, its being irregular, abrupt, like one of Elstir's mountains. It ought not to be too white then, but slightly yellowish, with that look of dull, dirty snow that Elstir's mountains have. The ice need not be at all big, only half an ice if you like, those lemon ices are still mountains, reduced to a tiny scale, but our imagination restores their dimensions, like those little Japanese dwarf trees which, one knows quite well, are still cedars, oaks, manchineels; so much so that if I arranged a few of them beside a little trickle of water in my room I should have a vast forest stretching down to a river, in which children would be lost. In the same way, at the foot of my yellowish lemon ice, I can see quite clearly postillions, travellers, post chaises over which my tongue sets to work to roll down freezing avalanches that will swallow them up" (the cruel delight with which she said this excited my jealousy); "just as," she went on, "I set my lips to work to destroy, pillar after pillar, those Venetian churches of a porphyry that is made with strawberries, and send what I spare of them crashing down upon the worshippers. Yes, all those monuments will pass from their stony state into my inside which throbs already with their melting coolness" (II, 468–69).

Norpois on Bergotte:

"Good heavens!" exclaimed M. de Norpois, inspiring me with doubts of my own intelligence far more serious than those that ordinarily distracted me, when I saw that what I valued a thousand thousand times more than myself, what I regarded as the most exalted thing in the world, was for him at the very foot of the scale of admiration. "I do not share your son's point of view. Bergotte is what I call a flute-player: one must admit that he plays on it very agreeably, although with a great deal of mannerism, of affectation. But when all is said, it is no more than that, and that is nothing very great. Nowhere does one find in his enervated writings anything that could be called construction. No action—or very little—but above all no range. His books fail at the foundation, or rather they have no foundation at all. At a time like the present, when the ever-increasing complexity of life leaves one scarcely a moment for reading, when the map of Europe has undergone radical alterations, and is on the eve, very probably, of undergoing others more drastic still, when so many new and threatening problems are arising on every side, you will allow me to suggest that one is entitled to ask that a writer should be something else than a fine intellect which makes us forget, amid otiose and byzantine discussions of the merits of pure form, that we may be overwhelmed at any moment by a double tide of barbarians, those from without and those from within our borders. I am aware that this is a blasphemy against the sacrosanct school of what these gentlemen term 'Art for Art's sake,' but at this period of history there are tasks more urgent than the manipulation of words in a harmonious manner. Not that Bergotte's manner is not now and then quite attractive. I have no fault to find with that, but taken as a whole, it is all very precious, very thin, and has very little virility. I can now understand more easily, when I bear in mind your altogether excessive regard for Bergotte, the few lines that you shewed me just now, which it would have been unfair to you not to overlook, since you yourself told me, in all simplicity, that they were merely a childish scribbling." (I had, indeed, said so, but I did not think anything of the sort.) (I, 362–63).

Robert Frost once gave a negative definition of poetry: it is, he said, what gets lost in translation. Probably something similar holds for humor. How much we must be missing by not reading the original! and not only so, but also this: how much we should be missing if we read the original, as we should have to do, only as students of French, not as native to its climate and customs.

Yet once that is granted we may go on to be a little grateful for the much that remains, which the translator has found means of preserving or, in certain instances of verbal play, found equivalents for.

This is a hard subject to discuss. Just as the teacher of poetry ought not to spend the class hour saying "Isn't that beautiful?" to students who possibly do not agree, so the idea of lecturing on the funniness of jokes has its appalling aspect. But hard or not, it is a subject, how funny Proust's world is even while being in the same breath so sorrowful, that demands an attention it almost never gets.

Since I began the lecture by putting Proust and Shakespeare in an admittedly rather odd relation, I shall make matters even worse now by quoting to you a beautiful sentence Dr. Johnson wrote about the Plays, and try to show how it brings out something about both Proustian comedy and Proustian narration in general. The Plays, says Dr. J.,

> are not, in the rigorous and critical sense, either tragedies or comedies, but compositions of a distinct kind; exhibiting the real state of sublunary nature, which partakes of good and evil, joy and sorrow, mingled with endless variety of proportion and innumerable modes of combination; and expressing the course of the world, in which the loss of one is the gain of another; in which at the same time, the reveler is hasting to his wine, and the mourner burying his friend; in which the malignity of one is sometimes defeated by the frolick of another; and many mischiefs and many benefits are done and hindered without design.

As I copied out that sentence it seemed that I saw it working even more exactly for Proust than for Shakespeare: consider the episode of the Duchess' red shoes in the light of that about the reveler and the mourner. But more than by particular comparisons I was struck by the general truth of the description, which may be brought out by a comparison.

Compared with Proust, almost any other novelist appears as single-mindedly linear in his composition. I am exaggerating, and of course there are exceptions, yet I think the exaggeration useful in making clear how very simple is the conventional way of telling a story, whereby the novelist works in almost a Euclidean manner, by demonstrations that one after another accumulate in force but that have each a unity and a certain independence.

For an example: in Jane Austen's *Sense and Sensibility,* immediately after the introduction of the characters and situation, there is a marvelous and uproarious second chapter consisting of one conversation between Mr. John Dashwood and his wife. His father has left him the whole estate but recommended most strongly, on his deathbed, that he take generous care of his mother and sisters; and he has agreed. The action of chapter two, then, is how Mrs. Dashwood, by easy stages and in a matter of only four pages, gets her husband down from giving his sisters a thousand pounds each to giving them nothing at all: "he finally resolved, that it would be absolutely unnecessary, if not highly indecorous, to do more for the widow and children of his father, than such kind of neighborly acts as his own wife pointed out."

Now this is a beautiful scene, and I wish there were time for the pleasure of reading it aloud to you. You will understand that by choosing such an example I am stressing that I do not mean this style of narrating is inferior to Proust's, but only that it is illuminating by its difference. For if you agree that Jane Austen's way of handling that episode is characteristic of method for most novelists you will appreciate what a strange thing Proust is attempting.

Jane Austen's chapter is single-minded, pointed, and terribly funny; that is, both terrible and funny, in its moral demonstration: this, it seems to say, is how normal, decent, nice people behave when money is involved; and if the behavior seems comically exaggerated, that is perhaps only because the entire sequence of stages of self-indulgence at the expense of others is compressed into one conversation, from which all other material is absolutely excluded.

X

The Dreyfus Case, and How Proust Uses It.

About the celebrated affair itself I shall be brief, if only because many of you probably are better acquainted with the facts than I am; which is in itself somewhat remarkable, for most treason trials are not so well or so long remembered by the children of nations having nothing at all to do with the matter in the first place. But, as Hannah Arendt tells us, a play on the subject, produced in France in 1931, engendered such effects of violence as might have been expected had the various trials been still going on; and she sums up: "The wrong done to a single Jewish officer in France was able to draw from the rest of the world a more vehement and united reaction than all the persecutions of German Jews a generation later."

The descriptions and opinions I shall set forth in what follows are drawn in the main from Hannah Arendt, *Origins of Totalitarianism,* chapter four: "The Dreyfus Affair"; from Barbara Tuchman, *The Proud Tower,* chapter four, "Give Me Combat!"; and from George D. Painter, *Proust: The Early Years,* chapter thirteen, "The Dreyfus Case." Also from some of the relevant passages of the novel itself, beginning with an intermittently heard conversation between Bloch and Norpois at the home of Mme. de Villeparisis:

M. de Norpois . . . spoke to Bloch with great affability of the terrible, perhaps fatal period through which France was passing. As this presumably meant that M. de Norpois (to whom Bloch had confessed his belief in the innocence of Dreyfus) was an ardent anti-Dreyfusard, the Ambassador's geniality, his air of tacit admission that his listener was in the right, of never doubting that they were both of the same opinion, of being prepared to join forces with him to overthrow the Government, flattered Bloch's vanity and aroused his curiosity. What were the important points which M. de Norpois never specified but on which he seemed implicitly to affirm that he was in agreement with Bloch; what opinion, then, did he hold of the case, that could bring them together? . . . He returned to the Dreyfus case, but did not succeed in elucidating M. de Norpois's own views. He tried to induce him to speak of the officers whose names were appearing constantly in the newspapers at that time; they aroused more curiosity than the politicians, well known already, but, wearing a special garb, emerging from the obscurity of a different kind of life and a religiously guarded silence, simply stood up and spoke and disappeared again, like Lohengrin landing from a skiff drawn by a swan. . . . To Bloch's questions M. de Norpois replied:

"There are two officers involved in the case now being tried of whom I remember hearing some time ago from a man in whose judgment I felt great confidence, and who praised them both highly—I mean M. de Miribel. They are Lieutenant-Colonel Henry and Lieutenant-Colonel Picquart."

"But," exclaimed Bloch, "the divine Athena, daughter of Zeus, has put in the mind of one the opposite of what is in the mind of the other. And they are fighting against one another like two lions. Colonel Picquart had a splendid position in the Army, but his Moira has led him to the side that was not rightly his. The sword of the Nationalists will carve his tender flesh, and he will be cast out as food for the beasts of prey and the birds that wax fat upon the bodies of men."

M. de Norpois made no reply. . . .

Bloch tried to pin M. de Norpois down on Colonel Picquart.

"There can be no two opinions," replied M. de Norpois, "his evidence had to be taken. I am well aware that, by maintaining this attitude, I have drawn screams of protest from more than one of my colleagues, but to my mind the Government were bound to let the Colonel speak. One can't dance lightly out of a blind alley like that, or if one does there's always the risk of falling into a ditch. As for the officer himself, his statement gave one, at the first hearing, a most excellent impression. When one saw him, looking so well in that smart Chasseur uniform, come into court and relate in a perfectly simple and frank tone what he had seen and what he had deduced, and say: 'On my honour as a soldier' " (here M. de Norpois's voice shook with a faint patriotic throb) " 'such is my conviction,' it is impossible to deny that the impression he made was profound."

"There; he is a Dreyfusard, there's not the least doubt of it," thought Bloch.

"But where he entirely forfeited all the sympathy that he had managed to attract was when he was confronted with the registrar, Gribelin. When one heard that old public servant, a man who had only one answer to make," (here M. de Norpois began to accentuate his words with the energy of his sincere convictions) "when one listened to him, when one saw him look his superior officer in the face, not afraid to hold his head up to him, and say to him in a tone that admitted of no response: 'Colonel, sir, you know very well that I have never told a lie, you know that at this moment, as always, I am speaking the truth,' the wind changed; M. Picquart might move heaven and earth at the subsequent hearings; he made a complete fiasco."

"No; evidently he's an anti-Dreyfusard; it's quite obvious," said Bloch to himself. "But if he considers Picquart a traitor and a liar, how can he take his revelations seriously, and quote them as if he found them charming and believed them to be sincere. And if, on the other hand, he sees in him an honest man easing his conscience, how can he suppose him to have been lying when he was confronted with Gribelin?" (I, 882–87)

What seems to me illuminating about the case was the manner in which it revealed that mysterious crossing place in human doings where fact shades into value, and where the literal shades into the symbolic. For it seems to have begun not as a criminal conspiracy by the French Intelligence services, but as an honest (and rather hasty) mistake, but one which could not be admitted after the fact, so that such evidence as could not be found had to be invented, and was.

In 1894 Captain Alfred Dreyfus was convicted of betraying military secrets to Germany; it was not, says Tuchman, a deliberate plot to frame an innocent man, but "the outcome of a reasonable suspicion acted on by dislike, some circumstantial evidence and instinctive prejudice" (p. 173). But compare Arendt where it is not so certain:

It has always remained somewhat obscure whether the arrest and condem-
nation of Dreyfus was simply a judicial error which just happened by chance
to light up a political conflagration, or whether the General Staff deliberately
planted the forged *bordereau* for the express purpose of at last branding a
Jew as a traitor. In favor of the latter hypothesis is the fact that Dreyfus was
the first Jew to find a post on the General Staff and under existing conditions
this could only have aroused not merely annoyance but positive fury and

> consternation. In any case anti-Jewish hatred was unleashed even before the
> verdict was returned (p. 104).

Apart from being a Jew, Dreyfus appears to have been both unat-
tractive and undistinguished, a thoroughly mediocre personality.

The prosecuting officers, unable to find sufficient information
of the type which at first justified the charge, forged what was
needed and was enough to convince the General Staff, yet not it
seemed enough for legal conviction. Hence the trial was held in
secret, and the forged evidence made available to the military judges
but not to the defense. And it was these two things, the secret trial
and the evidence withheld from Dreyfus' counsel, that were chiefly
responsible, at first among only a few persons, for the movement
for a new trial that came to be called Revision and Revisionism.
Meanwhile, Dreyfus was sentenced to life imprisonment in solitary
confinement on Devil's Island off the coast of what was then French
Guiana.

In all that followed, the actual question of the guilt or innocence of one man on a specific charge became merely the fulcrum
on which enormous forces swung and would not balance; but first,
as barely as possible, a few dates and facts.

1895: Colonel Picquard (or Picquart), becoming head of the
Information Division, tells the chief of General Staff Boisdeffre that
he believes Dreyfus innocent and a Major Walsin-Esterhazy guilty.
Presently Picquard is removed to a post in Tunisia, whence, in 1897
he informed the vice-president of the senate of his belief as to
Dreyfus' innocence. Whereupon Clemenceau began agitating for a
reexamination, Zola wrote *J'accuse*, Picquard was put under military arrest, and Zola was convicted on a charge of calumniating the
army. (See Painter, I, 277.)

1898: Esterhazy was dishonorably discharged for embezzle-
ment and told a British journalist that he, not Dreyfus, had written
the bordereau that had formed the first basis for the indictment; he
had forged it in Dreyfus' hand on instructions from a superior.
Whereupon in a few days Colonel (formerly Major) Henry confessed having forged other pieces of evidence for the secret trial and
then committed suicide. (Painter, I, 284)

1899: The Court of Appeals annulled the original 1894 sentence, and the revision trial took place. This trial did not acquit Dreyfus, but reduced his sentence to ten years because of extenuating circumstances. A week later Dreyfus was pardoned by the president of the Republic. Note that in all this Dreyfus has still not been exonerated, and in law he never was. The pardon was a solution to a threatened international boycott of the Paris Exposition of 1900, and as soon as that had successfully opened the Chamber of Deputies voted against any further revision, and six months later the whole affair was supposed to be buried forever by a general amnesty.

1903: Dreyfus appeals for a new revision. In 1906, when Clemenceau became prime minister, the Court of Appeals annulled the sentence of the revision trial of 1899 and acquitted Dreyfus of all charges, something it had no authority to do. Arendt concludes her account of the facts with a melancholy anecdote: "Nine years after the pardon and two years after Dreyfus was cleared, when, at Clemenceau's instance, the body of Emile Zola was transferred to the Pantheon, Alfred Dreyfus was openly attacked in the street. A Paris court acquitted his assailant and indicated that it 'dissented' from the decision which had cleared Dreyfus" (p. 90).

After so much in the way of "fact" we have to understand as simply as we may the immense complications, mysteries and intrigues that have to do with the symbolic, and with "values."

You will remember that France had undergone a revolution, and that at the time of Dreyfus this was roughly a century in the past, or as far away from the living as our own Civil War from ourselves today. That revolution, involving much destruction, violent frenzy, and a breakdown of civil order during successive insurrectionary regimes, was the opportunity of a young soldier Napoleon Bonaparte, who, beginning with Paris, restored order, invented and developed the grand army, and turned the new republic into a still newer French empire which in the form of that army spread victoriously across Europe until the flood reached Moscow and began to ebb. After Napoleon's final exile the empire was restored, only to be overthrown again by a republic. In still a further act of that great drama, the French army was conquered by the German empire in the year of our author's birth.

So that army had a double symbolic value in France; it was the memory of past greatness and the prophecy of renewed greatness, of revenge and of glory, of, in fact, 1914:

> In the eyes of the people the Army was above politics; it was the nation, it was France, it was the greatness of France. It was the Army of Revolution as of Empire, the Army of Valmy in '92 when Goethe, watching, said, "From this day forth commences a new era in the world's history." It was the Army of Marengo, Austerlitz and Wagram, the *Grande Armée* that Lavisse proudly called "one of the most perfect instruments of war history has ever seen"; the Army of the cuirasse and saber, of the kepi and *pantalons rouges*, of Sebastopol and the Malakoff, of Magenta and Solferino, the Army that had made France the greatest military power in Europe until the rise of Prussia, the Army of tragedy as of glory, the Army of the Last Cartridges at Sedan, of the wild cavalry charge that evoked the German Emperor's cry, "*Oh, les braves gens!*" Twenty-five years later, under the never-absent shadow of Germany, the Army was both defender of the nation and instrument of *revanche*. It was the means of restoring, someday, the national glory. Men lifted their hats when the colonel and the colors at the head of a regiment marched by. In the words of a character whom Anatole France was satirizing—though not misrepresenting—the Army "is all that is left of our glorious past. It consoles us for the present and gives us hope of the future." The Army was *les braves gens*. (Tuchman, p. 175)

Tuchman (again p. 175) does not think of the army as especially involved with the clergy, but Arendt differs (p. 101), saying that

> the army—left in a political vacuum by the Third Republic—gladly accepted the guidance of the Catholic clergy which at least provided for civilian leadership without which the military lose their "raison d'être" (which) is "to defend the principle embodied in civilian society"—as Clemenceau put it.
>
> The Catholic Church then owed its popularity to the widespread popular skepticism which saw in the republic and in democracy the loss of all order, security, and political will. To many the hierarchic system of the Church seemed the only escape from chaos. Indeed, it was this, rather than any religious revivalism, which caused the clergy to be held in respect. As a matter of fact, the staunchest supporters of the Church at that period were the exponents of that so-called "cerebral" Catholicism, the "Catholics without faith," who were henceforth to dominate the entire monarchist and extreme nationalist movement. Without believing in their other-worldly

basis, these "Catholics" clamored for more power to all authoritarian institutions (pp. 101–102).

The Church, especially the Jesuits, was monarchist and ancien régime, while the army was under the Republic.

The Jews, especially those of the rich middle class and those who had been in part accepted into society and even in the army, were of course involved because Dreyfus, being a Jew, was widely taken as representative.

Germany the great enemy was involved.

Finally, antisemitism was a new, nineteenth-century force that united segments of society otherwise having nothing much in common—the newspapers, the people, the mob, the upper classes, the Catholic middle class. Tuchman on newspapers:

> Variegated, virulent, turbulent, literary, inventive, personal, conscienceless and often vicious, the daily newspapers of Paris were the liveliest and most important element in public life. The dailies numbered between twenty-five and thirty-five at a given time. They represented every conceivable shade of opinion, calling themselves Republican, Conservative, Catholic, Socialist, Nationalist, Bonapartist, Legitimist, Independent, absolutely Independent, Conservative-Catholic, Conservative-Monarchist, Republican-Liberal, Republican-Socialist, Republican-Independent, Republican-Progressist, Republican-Radical-Socialist. . . . Only *Le Temps* in its eminence remained above the battle, although inclining gradually toward Revision. *Figaro*, following it in importance, proved vulnerable. Its editor, Fernand de Rodays, after hearing Dreyfus cry out his innocence on the occasion of his military degradation, believed him. Three years later he published the first evidence against Esterhazy as well as Zola's first articles. Although he was a father and father-in-law of officers, his enraged colleagues of the Nationalist press denounced him as a traducer of the Army and organized a campaign to cancel subscriptions to *Figaro*. The management succumbed and De Rodays was ousted, an affair of such moment that Paris gossip said he had been paid 400,000 francs to support Dreyfus and the management 500,000 to get rid of him (pp. 178–79).

Tuchman on antisemitism:

> The sudden and malign bloom of anti-Semitism in France was part of a wider outbreak. As a social and political force anti-Semitism emerged in the late Nineteenth Century out of other expanding forces which were building tensions between classes and among nations. Industrialization, imperialism, the growth of cities, the decline of the countryside, the power of money and the power of machines, the clenched fist of the working class, the red flag of

Socialism, the wane of the aristocracy, all these forces and factors were churning like the bowels of a volcano about to erupt. "Something very great—ancient, cosmopolitan, feudal, agrarian Europe," as a contemporary said, was dying and in the process creating conflicts, fears and newfound strengths that needed outlet.

A classic outlet was anti-Semitism (p. 182).

Arendt on society, politicians, and the mob:

The mob is primarily a group in which the residue of all classes are represented. This makes it so easy to mistake the mob for the people, which also comprises all strata of society. While the people in all great revolutions fight for true representation, the mob always will shout for the "strong man," the "great leader." For the mob hates society from which it is excluded, as well as Parliament where it is not represented. Plebiscites, therefore, with which modern mob leaders have obtained such excellent results, are an old concept of politicians who rely upon the mob. . . .

High society and politicians of the Third Republic had produced the French mob in a series of scandals and public frauds. They now felt a tender sentiment of parental familiarity with their offspring, a feeling mixed with admiration and fear. The least society could do for its offspring was to protect it verbally. While the mob actually stormed Jewish shops and assailed Jews in the streets, the language of high society made real, passionate violence look like harmless child's play. . . . The upper classes knew that the mob was flesh of their flesh and blood of their blood. Even a Jewish historian of the time, although he had seen with his own eyes that Jews are no longer safe when the mob rules the street, spoke with secret admiration of the "great collective movement." This only shows how deeply most Jews were rooted in a society which was attempting to eliminate them (p. 107).

One odd result of the case. Theodore Herzl, Paris correspondent for a Vienna paper, hearing the crowd at Dreyfus' degradation shrieking "Death to the Jews," went home and inside eighteen months organized the first Zionist Congress; so that the existence today of the state of Israel is connected directly with the Dreyfus case.

In this brief and superficial overview I, who am not a historian, and have had to take up a few saliencies at tenth-hand, have limited myself to the skeletal chronology of what happened in what succession and to the barest mention of the forces involved. You may read, in the sources I have cited (who will refer you to primary sources as well as to other secondary accounts, in great plenty), something of the frightful complexity generated by even the smallest happening to an individual, when such a happening involves directly and intimately, and so very revealingly, the institutions of human societies and the assumptions beneath these. And for a view of the rather frightening similarities such ritual dramas may have in every modern state some of you may want to compare the treason trial in the United States, some fifteen years ago, of Julius and Ethel Rosenberg.

If history repeats itself, that may be because historians do.

Meanwhile, however, I had best get back to our author.

In Proust's handling of the Dreyfus case, none of what I have outlined is explained or made explicit; all of it, and much more, is assumed. Through the middle sections of the novel, that is, "The Guermantes Way" and "Cities of the Plain," allusions and references come and go and return. The Affaire is perhaps the principal means of depicting social change, or one of two principal means, the other being homosexuality. Both offer views of how the high and the low in society are as it were reflected in one another as in distorting mirrors, a point made explicitly in the grandmother's remark about the "marquise" who runs the public toilet in the Champs-Elysées: "Could anything have been more typical of the Guermantes, or the Verdurins and their little circle?" Indeed, as the novel progresses toward its end, there is a section in which one sees clearly that, in both politics and society, and with reference to social change, the limited is replaced by the unlimited, the Dreyfus case by the war and the fashionable parties by surreptitious gatherings at a brothel for male prostitutes.

For as Proust sees the Dreyfus case it is comparable in the social realm to those complicated associations of images I have pointed to as characterizing his descriptive reflections; that is, it unites so large a collection of disparates—Jews, aristocrats, bourgeoisie both high and low, Catholics, the army—as to be able to produce rather fantastic modifications in all social and hierarchical arrangements.

For example: Odette, because she remains antisemitic and anti-Dreyfus although married to a Jew, gains a reputation for lofty and disinterested patriotism.

For example again, the chief meaning of the Dreyfus case for Basin duc de Guermantes is that by devious indirections it caused him not to be elected president of the jockey club; for this result he blames chiefly his friendship with Swann, though perhaps Saint-Loup as well may have been responsible, he being a Dreyfusard just as the Duke was coming up for election to the club, though his political attitude is owing to—and lasts only as long as—his attachment to Rachel.

For Swann himself, his Dreyfusism causes the rumor to be spread at the Prince de Guermantes' party that he has been disgraced and that the Prince has forbidden him the house; the reality, as Marcel hears it from Swann himself in a long and circumstantial anecdote several times interrupted (II, 76–81), is quite the opposite: both the Prince and his wife, unbeknownst to each other, have become partisans of Dreyfus' innocence, and this has been revealed to them by their confessor; that is what the Prince called Swann in to tell him. But on the other hand, Swann's conviction of the innocence of Dreyfus does not turn him against the army, which he reveres; so he refuses to sign a petition by Bloch, feeling that his name is too Jewish not to create a bad effect: "with the result that, if he passed in the eyes of many people as a fanatical Dreyfusard, (Bloch) found him lukewarm, infected with Nationalism, and a militarist" (I, 83).

The general conclusion: "In reality we always discover afterwards that our adversaries had a reason for being on the side they espoused, which has nothing to do with any element of right that there may be on that side" (I, 82).

I should like to say that the poet, among his many false and arbitrary dreams, sometimes dreams a true dream; true at least in the sense that it is presently realized. This realization belongs to science, though that should not be thought of as a limitation on science, condemning it only to implementing the dreams of poets, for science dreams its own dreams also, and very poetical, in the best sense, some of them are. Better to say, perhaps, that this realization belongs to the life of action, in which science, politics, religion, education, all to a certain extent share.

This is not easy to illustrate, this proposition about an occasional true dream, whose truth appears when it is realized in the waking world, the world of action and practical result. Freud found his Oedipal theme in a play by Sophocles, that's well known; or else when he had isolated and described empirically a more-or-less consistent form in mental life he recognized its image in Oedipus and gave this form the name of the Oedipus complex. I should like an illustration a little more technically decisive, a little more demonstrative in detail, and was fortunate enough to come across one. It is only one, true. But after what we have said about exceptions and the exceptional* I do not think we are entitled to reject it.

Wilder Penfield describes certain by-effects of operations for forms of epilepsy,†

> The patient might exclaim in sudden surprise that he heard music, or that he heard a well-known person speaking, or that he saw something he had seen before, or that he was himself taking part in a former experience in which he was himself an actor.
>
> At such times the patient continued to be aware of the fact that he lay upon the operating room table, and yet the recollection continued, in spite of himself, as long as the electrode was kept in place, to vanish instantly when the electrode was withdrawn. . . .
>
> A South African who was being operated upon cried out in great surprise that he heard his cousins talking, and he explained that he seemed to be laughing there with them although he knew he was really in the operating room in Montreal. . . .
>
> It may be assumed then that in this area of cortex each successive conscious experience is laid down in a relatively permanent pattern of nerve-cell connections that records all those things of which a man is conscious at any given time. It is as though the cortex contained a continuous strip of cinematographic film, a strip that includes the waking record from childhood onward.

On the experience of recognizing an old friend after ten or twenty years:

> These are not portraits of still life; they are strips of action, each one as long as the periods of time during which you focussed your attention upon him. . . .

---

*See "Exceptions and Rules," in my *Figures of Thought* (Boston, 1978), 42–48.

† It is in part illuminating to compare Penfield's description of a similar phenomenon in brain surgery: "Some Observations on the Functional Organization of the Human Brain," *Smithsonian Annual Report*, 1955. The comparison is noticed by Dr. Merle Miller in *Nostalgia*, a book about Proust, but he doesn't develop the hint.

Patients often say, "this is not a memory, it is more vivid than that."

It may be that a reprojection of impulses back from the temporal cortex to the centroencephalic system occurs invariably like a reflection in a mirror, a reflection of which the individual takes cognizance. That may seem an extraordinary hypothesis, and yet if stimulation with a simple electrical current can recreate a total experience, the reflection mechanism exists. The neurone record is there and the records of previous similar experiences are there also so that judgments of familiarity and strangeness may be made and other elaborative processes. I suggest that reflection or reverberation back into the centroencephalic or integrative circuits must occur normally.

Compare Marcel on tasting the madeleine steeped in tea:

Will it ultimately reach the clear surface of consciousness, this memory, this old, dead moment which the magnetism of an identical moment has travelled so far to importune, to disturb, to raise up out of the very depths of my being? . . .

And suddenly the memory returns. . . .

And just as the Japanese amuse themselves by filling a porcelain bowl with water and steeping in it little crumbs of paper which until then are without character or form, but, the moment they become wet, stretch themselves and bend, take on color and distinctive shape, become flowers or houses or people, permanent and recognizable, so in that instant all the flowers in our garden and in M. Swann's park, and the water lilies on the Vivonne and the good folk of the village and their little dwellings and the parish church and the whole of Combray and of its surroundings, taking their proper shapes and growing solid, sprang into being, town and gardens alike, from my cup of tea (I, 35–36).

It seems to me clear enough that Wilder Penfield is not thinking about Proust, and probably has not read Proust; he came at a remarkably similar phenomenon by a remarkably different route; yet, just as in Proust's novel, Swann's Way and the Guermantes Way turned out after many years to be two ways of getting to the same place, even though they started out in opposite directions.

One observation to make about this coincidence is a tragic one concerning the human condition. The fairy godmother says over the infant's cradle, He may have one Freudian wish. It is proverbial that we get what we want in such a way that we are certain not to want it when we get it. And so to realize a dream is to deprive it of some of its power over the soul, to deprive it, most notably, of its charm. Leaving the realm of poetry, it enters the realm of prose (I am not talking about technical distinctions) and will never mean so much again. On the other hand, you can now do real things with it. The experience of Penfield's patients, written up in Penfield's style, carries with it nothing whatsoever of the melancholy delight of Marcel's experience written in the style of Marcel Proust. The imagination does not care.

But on the other hand, again, Penfield's surgery was not designed to give the patients back their past, but to cure their malady; the result he describes is a side-effect, though an extremely interesting one.

And, not to leave it at that, perhaps one could say this story is not over. For Penfield gives us, so to say, a new terminology with which we may reflect back on Proust, as well as reflecting also on other areas of human experience and knowledge. For in his prosy way Penfield asserts the technical, potentially the measurable and controllable equivalent of Proust's dream of joyful certainty in the overcoming of time; he suggests to us that among the billions of connections in the brain all our experience really is still present, living while we live, that nothing is lost and nothing passes away. What may be the results of a thought of this kind when once it ceases to be a poetical or religious vision and emerges in the austere and immensely powerful syntax of scientific statement, perhaps no man can say any more or better than I can. It ceases to be imaginative as it ceases to be imaginary. And it becomes instrumental, or operational, it enters a world on which it may have, one day, measurable though immense effects. One might say of it, that it is only an exception at present; but an exception on the point of proving a rule.*

*Alas, persons qualified both theoretically and practically in various branches of neuroscience tell me that no one, whether accidentally or on purpose, has ever duplicated Penfield's results. So my analogy remains just that, analogy, a more or less interesting fairy tale, though one from which, it is fair to suppose, some even stranger hypothesis may one day emerge to be tested.

XI

Proustian Narration.

The title of the chapter is "Mme. Swann at Home."
But Proust is in no hurry to get there, and it is not for fifty pages
or more that the narrator receives from Gilberte the invitation
which realizes his social and amatory dream. In order to illustrate
some traits of Proust's distinctive way of composition, I shall
summarize and comment upon the order and import of his considerations during those fifty or so pages. Most summarily, they are
about how Marcel was first allowed to go to the theater to hear the
great actress Berma, and what he thought about this experience;
also about how his father decided that he might after all be allowed
to become a writer. Both these permissions come about through
the more or less accidental intervention of an old diplomat, M. de
Norpois. Beginning at the beginning (I, 331) here is how it goes.

1. On having Norpois to dinner. Reputations have changed;
Cottard's has risen, while Swann's has fallen. Explanation of the
social results of Swann's marriage, with general reflection on character and action in which Swann is compared to a great artist who
late in life takes to, say, cooking or gardening. Similar explanation
of Cottard's rise: note the introductory sentence: "As for Cottard,
we shall meet him again and can study him at our leisure"—the
sort of interposition that, as some of you have remarked to me,
becomes increasingly frequent as the novel progresses and its long

lines of force become clear. Cottard's new dignity and impassivity remarked, I, 333.

2. Who was Norpois? Summary of his career, reflections on political advancement and influence in general. His character: governmental. His friendship with Marcel's father. King Theodosius. Marcel's mother's opinion of Norpois.

3. Time relations I, 336–37: The evening M. Norpois dined with the family follows the afternoon at the theater. It is during a year when Marcel still played in the Champs-Elysées and came to a realization concerning Gilberte and her parents. The New Year holidays. Because he is depressed about not being able to see Gilberte, his mother says that his father may let him go to hear Berma in the company of the grandmother. This however turns out to be on account of a passing remark by Norpois to the father. The same sort of remark has led to another consequence: Marcel may now become a writer instead of a diplomat; the father's views of "influence": ". . . as he had a certain amount of influence himself, he imagined that there was nothing that could not be 'arranged,' no problem for which a happy solution might not be found in the conversation of people who 'counted' " (I, 337–38).

4. Marcel tries to write something that will impress Norpois, but does not succeed. He dreams of hearing Berma in something "classic," and meditates upon how it is possible to judge of the greatness of the actress' art.

5. The doctor is against his going to the theater (I, 340) just as the grandmother had been (I, 337). Marcel reflects on the results he desires from the performance in balance with the illness he may expect: he demands "something different from pleasure; a series of verities pertaining to a world more real than that in which I lived." His expectations are informed by Bergotte's pamphlet which Gilberte has loaned him: Jansenist pallor, solar myth, etc. (I, 340).

6. His parents' permission, and Marcel's reflections thereupon, its twists and turns and intricate subtleties:

> In the first place, whereas I had been detesting them for their cruelty, their consent made them now so dear to me that the thought of causing them pain stabbed me also with a pain through which the purpose of life shewed itself as the pursuit not of truth but of loving-kindness, and life itself seemed good

or evil only as my parents were happy or sad. "I would rather not go, if it hurts you," I told my mother, who, on the contrary, strove hard to expel from my mind any lurking fear that she might regret my going, since that, she said, would spoil the pleasure that I should otherwise derive from *Phèdre*, and it was the thought of my pleasure that had induced my father and her to reverse their earlier decision. But then this sort of obligation to find a pleasure in the performance seemed to me very burdensome. Besides, if I returned home ill, should I be well again in time to be able to go to the Champs-Elysées as soon as the holidays were over and Gilberte returned? Against all these arguments I set, so as to decide which course I should take, the idea, invisible there behind its veil, of the perfections of Berma. I cast into one pan of the scales "Making Mamma unhappy," "risking not being able to go on the Champs-Elysées," and the other, "Jansenist pallor," "Solar myth," until the words themselves grew dark and clouded in my mind's vision, ceased to say anything to me, lost all their force; and gradually my hesitations became so painful that if I had now decided upon the theatre it would have been only that I might bring them to an end, and be delivered from them once and for all (I, 340–41).

He is finally decided in favor of going to the theater by the sight of the playbill, "whipped on by the magic words which now had taken the place in my mind, of 'Jansenist pallor' and 'Solar myth'; 'Ladies will not be admitted to the stalls in hats. The doors will be closed at two o'clock.' "

So. Ten pages have been taken up in a way that no self-respecting novelist ought to do, with reflections on people who are not even to appear in the scene when it gets going (Swann, Cottard), with multiple comparisons, interventions of strange materials, digressions. And yet in this style they are not digressions, they are the action itself. Somewhat as in Shakespeare's strange and wonderful *Troilus and Cressida*, the ways in which the action for the most part defers itself and gets lost turn out to be the action.

This is so because for Proust there is almost no such thing as the present; we live only in anticipation and memory, most of our days on earth, and the other names for anticipation and memory are desire and regret. It is anxiety, on the one hand, and remorse, on the other, that are able to unfold whole complex worlds from a single instant, and this—how imagination makes reality before experiencing it, and later tries for the most part vainly to put the two together—is Proust's real subject: artistic vision, artistic creation, in themselves.

So what he sacrifices in linear narration is made up for by his radical, exfoliating method, which is as it were that of a tree that branches as it grows, yet is still one thing; or like a fountain, in which the millions of drops form a single jet; or a jet which is itself something like a tree (see Proust's description of the fountain of Hubert Robert, which is a description of the art work as well as of the composition of society):

In a clearing surrounded by fine trees several of which were as old as itself, set in a place apart, one could see it in the distance, slender, immobile, stiffened, allowing the breeze to stir only the lighter fall of its pale and quivering plume. The eighteenth century had refined the elegance of its lines, but, by fixing the style of the jet, seemed to have arrested its life; at this distance one had the impression of a work of art rather than the sensation of water. The moist cloud itself that was perpetually gathering at its crest preserved the character of the period like those that in the sky assemble round the palaces of Versailles. But from a closer view one realised that, while it respected, like the stones of an ancient palace, the design traced for it beforehand, it was a constantly changing stream of water that, springing upwards and seeking to obey the architect's traditional orders, performed them to the letter only by seeming to infringe them, its thousand separate bursts succeeding only at a distance in giving the impression of a single flow. This was in reality as often interrupted as the scattering of the fall, whereas from a distance it had appeared to me unyielding, solid, unbroken in its continuity. From a little nearer, one saw that this continuity, apparently complete, was assured, at every point in the ascent of the jet, wherever it must otherwise have been broken, by the entering into line, by the lateral incorporation of a parallel jet which mounted higher than the first and was itself, at an altitude greater but already a strain upon its endurance, relieved by a third. Seen close at hand, drops without strength fell back from the column of water crossing on their way their climbing sisters and, at times, torn, caught in an eddy of the night air, disturbed by this ceaseless flow, floated awhile before being drowned in the basin. They teased with their hesitations, with their passage in the opposite direction, and blurred with their soft vapour the vertical tension of that stem, bearing aloft an oblong cloud composed of a thousand tiny drops, but apparently painted in an unchanging, golden brown which rose, unbreakable, constant, urgent, swift, to mingle with the clouds in the sky. Unfortunately, a gust of wind was enough to scatter it obliquely on the ground; at times indeed a single jet, disobeying its orders, swerved and, had they not kept a respectful distance, would have drenched to their skins the incautious crowd of gazers (II, 43).

Valéry put the process the other way round when he said: "Proust divides—and gives us the idea that he might go on dividing indefinitely—what other writers skip."

To which I add this observation: already, only about one-sixth the way into the whole work, we find it has become and is becoming its own memory, its own history, its own archaeology even. A new character is introduced, M. de Norpois; but he is introduced into strangely familiar circumstances. A visitor comes to the family home, he is accidentally the cause of Marcel's having his own way, but a way which is deleterious to his health, makes his mother and grandmother unhappy, and which consequently is attended by considerable guilt. It is, in short, the episode of the good-night kiss all over again, varied now by age and other particulars but nevertheless clearly informing "real life" with its archetypal pattern. One may add that now the guilt about the mother is associated with art in the figure of Berma, a great actress, playing the role of a mother illicitly in love with her son.

One reason for my choosing this episode as illustrative is that now, having read so much further than it, we can see something of its lines to the future as well as its background in the past. For almost no one in Proust is allowed to drop out of the novel, even though many persons disappear for years, for hundreds of pages. Norpois, for instance, introduced in the passage we are examining, arouses Marcel's hope that he will speak favorably of him to Mme. Swann, but Marcel learns from this the typical Proustian lesson: Norpois sees this hope and accordingly will do nothing to satisfy it; Norpois turns out to be the lover of Mme. de Villeparisis, and so leads to the Guermantes, where Marcel learns that Norpois has said a vicious thing about him (he learns this, by an exact turn, from Mme. Swann); toward the end of the novel Norpois is seen with Mme. de Villeparisis dining in Venice; both of them in doddering old age; and Norpois' elaborately phrased and inaccurate political commentaries are still echoing during the war.

Berma, again, seen now but as an actress on the stage, enters the novel for a terrible few moments far in the future: she is ruined in health by the financial requirements of her daughter and son-in-law, which compel her to return to the stage; they desert her to go cadge an invitation to the Princess de Guermantes' party from of all people Rachel, who by telling Berma of this disgrace brings about her death; of which Proust remarks: "great actresses are frequently the victims of family conspiracies woven about them, as so often happens in the denouement of the tragedies in which they acted" (II, 1100)

I defer further comment on method until we have gone further with the episode itself.

7. Typically, the end of anticipation is the beginning of regret: "Alas! that matinée was to prove a bitter disappointment." As typically, that announcement is succeeded by an extended description of Françoise's preparations for the dinner which is to follow, in which she is compared with Michaelangelo; yet even this digression is drawn into relevance by one pointed remark: "if Françoise was consumed by the burning certainty of creative genius, my lot was the cruel anxiety of the seeker after truth."

8. At last we are in the theater (I, 342). Marcel speaks constantly of his pleasure, his happiness, which however are entirely in anticipation: "The last moments of my pleasure were during the opening scenes of *Phèdre*." There are some marvelous touches: the discovery for example that there was but one stage for everybody, the astonishment at the entrance of the two men "who must have been very angry with each other," his fear that Berma might act badly because of the rudeness of the audience, his mistaking the first two actresses to appear for Berma. His desperate efforts to realize in the present what he is experiencing (I, 344), the binoculars (I, 345), his disappointment at her rendering of the speech to Hippolyte on which he had been counting so much (I, 345). His admiration is evoked by the applause; emotion of the crowd, that "aura" which surrounds momentous happenings. "The more I applauded, the better, it seemed to me, did Berma act."

9. Marcel is introduced to M. de Norpois (I, 346). Norpois on literature, especially the very funny passage about the son of a friend:

"There is the case of the son of one of my friends, which, *mutatis mutandis*, is very much like yours. . . . He too has chosen to leave the Quai d'Orsay, although the way had been paved for him there by his father, and without caring what people might say, he has settled down to write. And certainly, he's had no reason to regret it. He published two years ago—of course, he's much older than you, you understand—a book dealing with the Sense of the Infinite on the Western Shore of Victoria Nyanza, and this year he has brought out a little thing, not so important as the other, but very brightly, in places perhaps almost too pointedly written, on the Repeating Rifle in the Bulgarian Army; and these have put him quite in a class by himself" (I, 347).

Norpois on the father's investments:

You would have supposed, to hear him, that he attributed to the relative values of investments, and even to investments themselves, something akin to aesthetic merit. Of one, comparatively recent and still little known, which my father mentioned, M. de Norpois, like the people who have always read the books of which, you imagine, you yourself alone have ever heard, said at once, "Ah, yes, I used to amuse myself for some time with watching it in the papers; it was quite interesting," with the retrospective smile of a regular subscriber who has read the latest novel already, in monthly instalments, in his magazine (I, 348).

and one begins to see retrospectively the way in which a great deal of this episode is composed, for the idea of art is constantly being played off against the idea of worldliness and opinion. Norpois' literary criticism comes in the same terms as his appreciation of investments and his speech about Berma's acting (I, 350) and his appreciation of Françoise's cooking and his remarks about diplomacy (I, 352ff). Marcel's puzzled comment on Norpois' tastes:

M. de Norpois, so as to add his own contribution to the gaiety of the repast, entertained us with a number of the stories with which he was in the habit of regaling his colleagues in "the career," quoting now some ludicrous sentence uttered by a politician, an old offender, whose sentences were always long and packed with incoherent images, now some monumental epigram of a diplomat, sparkling with attic salt. But, to tell the truth, the criterion which for him set apart these two kinds of phrase in no way resembled that which I was in the habit of applying to literature. Most of the finer shades escaped me; the words which he repeated with derision seemed to me not to differ very greatly from those which he found remarkable. He belonged to the class of men who, had we come to discuss the books that I liked, would have said: "So you understand that, do you? I must confess that I do not understand, I am not initiated;" but I could have matched his attitude, for I did not grasp the wit or folly, the eloquence or pomposity which he found in a statement or a speech, and the absence of any perceptible reason for one's being badly and the other's well expressed made that sort of literature seem more mysterious, more obscure to me than any other. I could distinguish only that to repeat what everybody else was thinking was, in politics, the mark not of an inferior but of a superior mind (I, 351–52).

M. de Norpois' style of speech, composed entirely of clichés (I, 354). His opinion of Balbec (I, 356). His opinion of Mme. Swann and of Swann's marriage (I, 356–58).

10. This is followed by a critical examination of love and marriage (I, 358–61), in which the voice is clearly that of the old Marcel who is telling the story, not of the young one who is living it.

11. Norpois on the opinion of the Comte de Paris concerning Odette (I, 362). His criticism of Bergotte, literary (I, 362–64) and personal (I, 364–65).

12. Mention of Mme. Swann and Gilberte. Marcel's gratitude, impulse to kiss M. de Norpois' "gentle hands, white and crumpled, which looked as though they had been left lying too long in water." On his learning how M. de Norpois had noticed this impulse, and all the complexities of association and memory that surround the anecdote:

> . . . some years later, in a house in which M. de Norpois, who was also calling there, had seemed to me the most solid support that I could hope to find, because he was the friend of my father, indulgent, inclined to wish us all well, and besides, by his profession and upbringing, trained to discretion, when, after the Ambassador had gone, I was told that he had alluded to an evening long ago when he had seen the moment in which I was just going to kiss his hands, not only did I colour up to the roots of my hair but I was stupefied to learn how different from all that I had believed were not only the manner in which M. de Norpois spoke of me but also the constituents of his memory: this tittle-tattle enlightened me as to the incalculable proportions of absence and presence of mind, of recollection and forgetfulness which go to form the human intelligence; and I was as marvellously surprised as on the day on which I read for the first time, in one of Maspero's books, that we had an exact list of the sportsmen whom Assurbanipal used to invite to his hunts, a thousand years before the Birth of Christ (I, 366).

13. Marcel's request of Norpois (I, 366), and its results (I, 367).

14. The newspaper account of Berma's performance, and Marcel's response to it (I, 368–69).

15. Reflection on the flight of time (Compare Rilke in *Malte Laurids Brigge*) in one's life, and in the novel (I, 369–70).

16. The family imitates Norpois' way of speaking. Françoise as artist (I, 371).

And that may fairly be called the end of the episode, for on the next page New Year's Day has come, etc.

After a summary so detailed as to have been, possibly, somewhat tedious, I ask now if any general reflections are to be made.

If you will remember, to use as a model, the Jane Austen scene I used a while back, you can see something of Proust's remarkable differences from other novelists. He rarely aims at a single effect, that's one thing, and when Marcel aims at a single effect (to get M. de Norpois to speak of him to Odette) he fails, as usual. And yet the whole scene, composed of so many elements, has a coherency of its own, and this is partly because, as I observed before, the novel has already become its own memory, and ours as well.

This is so simple a point that it might easily be overlooked; yet it is odd. In most sorts of fictional narrative it would be out of place for the author, even through the voice of a character, to do literary criticism. As Stendhal said of introducing politics, it would be like a pistol shot in the middle of a concert. Only there is this difference, that the literary criticism here is of Bergotte, who is already a character in the novel. As the world of the book gradually expands from the room in Combray to take in Paris and the great world of society, it does so particularly by this echoing, resonant, returning method, whereby people and their doings are considered from a good many points of view; and by these intermittences and returns Proust is imperceptibly building in our own minds the idea of his world as always enlarging yet always self-contained: it is not too much to say that one law of his composition is this: no matter how exclusive the people—such as Oriane, whose theme song is that she "simply doesn't know" this one, that one and the other one—everyone in this book either knows everyone else or will know everyone else. In fact, the great "actions" of the book, the critical stages on its way, consist quite simply of introductions, and these usually though not always take place at parties. For introductions mark the dramatic moments of social change, the demonstration of which is one of the great objects of the work; so this scene, consisting largely of the introduction of Marcel to Norpois, has for Marcel the object of a further introduction, to Mme. Swann, as we have seen (and for his father, we learn at another place, it has the object also of an introduction, for he wants Norpois to propose him for the Academy of Moral Sciences).

Another law of composition: the method is gossip.

People in Proust rarely have by their actions any direct effect on the actions of others (except possibly a negative effect; a character may well refrain from doing something when he knows it would please another character); they talk endlessly and wonderfully about each other, but all this talk rarely issues in action. Great changes at last do come about, but it is only in odd instances that they can be referred, when they happen, to one event in particular; rather, we are enabled by Proust's refinement of vision, which does for time what the telescope does for space, to see society as a perpetual process of accretion, erosion, and interchange, brought about by agencies working as steadily and minutely as wind, water, and sand do on terrain.

Now the episode of fifty pages that we have been inspecting is made coherent in a number of ways. First, we ought to acknowledge the brilliance and skill of the texture itself, the local and minute triumphs of observation, mimicry, imaginative re-creation, wide-ranging association, analysis, that keep it all continuously interesting; we are in touch, at the very surface of the thing, with the liveliest of sensibilities, who meets at every point Henry James's counsel of perfection for the novelist: "Try to be one of the persons upon whom nothing is lost."

Then there is the figure of Norpois himself, who dominates the action, or inaction, for three-fifths of the time. He is the Polonius of the novel, "full of high sentence, but a bit obtuse," shrewd, short-sighted, pompous, complacent, and drawn with marvelous art. In general, however broad the comic treatment of some of the persons, there is a great subtlety in Proust's knack of getting their style of talk—when he comes to exhibit (and for a hundred pages or so) the wit of the Guermantes, you observe how neatly Oriane's examples of this celebrated wit are just witty enough to pass for miraculous in her circle even while they are just plain not witty enough for the reader to be drawn into that circle.

In the midst of the high comedy involved in the presentation of Norpois before the admiration of the father, the suppressed and deferential skepticism of the mother, the deadpan naivety of Marcel as foil to all this, and even before Françoise's estimate of him on grounds rather of age than of his position as ambassador ("He's a good old soul, like me," she says), much that is serious and dark is also going forward. For in the devastating portrait of this old man, this old politician, is also a savage critique of worldliness, of stupidity in power, of the corruption of language liberated from the restraining influence of thought, of the hopelessly triumphant smugness that was all unconsciously leading the nations of Europe into madness during the couple of decades between the Dreyfus case and the World War; for real-life imitations of Norpois you might well look at Barbara Tuchman's *The Guns of August.*

But beneath or behind these novelistic triumphs there is the thematic coherency of music. Practically everything of importance in the episode has to do with style. For the novelist who is going to wind up his great work with the flat opinion that Art is the Last Judgment is also the young man just growing into the world, touchingly and humorously anxious to learn what is fine, beautiful, true, always inquiring of the wise who expose in their answers not only that they are not wise but that for them, art, far from being the last judgment or anything like it, is a civilized amusement upon which they bring to bear the same cultivated "taste" that enters into their judgments also of manners, morals, fashion, politics, even money.

This theme having to do with style poses insistently what is in two senses a critical question: how do we connect our impressions with our opinions? In two senses, for as well as being decisive for Marcel's growing up and discovery of his vocation, it is decisive for literary criticism. For on the one hand you have the mere unadorned art work, a masterpiece, *Hamlet,* say; while on the other you have the learned world and the fashionable world (not so far apart in this respect as they may otherwise seem) where *Hamlet* is described as a masterpiece because it is alleged to obey certain—rather mysterious—laws of dramaturgy, in spite of the fact that obedience to these laws has helped many a playwright to produce potboilers. In somewhat the same way, the conservatories of Europe and America for a couple of centuries taught counterpoint according to rules and principles learned from the works of J. S. Bach; though from the results, one would have to allow that maybe J. S. Bach had not paid much attention to those rules and principles which his fugues were later said to exemplify.

In somewhat the same way, again, Marcel tries to connect his experience of Berma with principles of dramatic art; but while he can experience the secondhand charm of a description giving him the elegant counters of Jansenist pallor and solar myth, he cannot experience these epithets, or indeed much of anything at all, in the acting of Berma.

Indeed, it may be that the project, at least in that form, is a hopeless one; if so, we teachers and students at a university ought to learn the fact at once, for we spend ever so much of our time in just that enterprise, the putting together of experienced phenomena with laws.

The partial resolution of the question, How do we connect our impressions with our opinions? is not to be found in the scene we have been examining. As it becomes decisive for love as well as for art, the answer, if it is an answer, is long deferred. Yet we do get one stage further, and typically it is four hundred pages further on that we do so, when Marcel, now a young man, goes to hear Berma in *Phèdre* again.

It should be remarked, by the way, that in reading thus discontinuously for once, we get a fine impression of the sureness with which the stages of Marcel's development are marked and detailed. Now he is no longer a boy, but a young man; no longer eager and puzzled, but extremely sophisticated, already worldly and somewhat bored. And it is of moment to note that this second visit to the theater is not to be read in a simple way as the triumphant resolution of the bewilderments occasioned by the first: Marcel is indeed able to "understand" what makes Berma supreme to the point of miracle, but only because her art, and art in general, have become less important to him, have become, though at a higher pitch of intelligence, more what they were for M. de Norpois.

Still, he has learned something, or maybe better say he has unlearned some false expectations that he had earlier entertained. He is a stage further on, he is able to appreciate Berma's perfection, not in terms of an abstract formula, but as and for itself. The brilliancies of technique which might have enabled the younger Marcel to understand that he was in the presence of genius he now understands to be the marks of the second rate:

> I no longer felt the same indulgence as on the former occasion towards the deliberate expressions of affection or anger which I had then remarked in the delivery and gestures of Aricie, Ismène and Hippolyte. It was not that the players—they were the same, by the way—did not still seek, with the same intelligent application, to impart now a caressing inflexion, or a calculated ambiguity to their voices, now a tragic amplitude, or a suppliant meekness to their movements. Their intonations bade the voice: "Be gentle, sing like a nightingale, caress and woo"; or else, "now wax furious," and then hurled themselves upon it, trying to carry it off with them in their frenzied rush. But it, mutinous, independent of their diction, remained unalterably their natural voice with its material defects or charms, its everyday vulgarity or affectation, and thus presented a sum-total of acoustic or social phenomena which the sentiment contained in the lines they were repeating was powerless to alter (I, 746).

Berma, in contrast, succeeds by disappearing:

> . . . the talent of Berma, which had evaded me when I sought so greedily to seize its essential quality, now, after these years of oblivion, in this hour of indifference, imposed itself, with all the force of a thing directly seen, on my admiration. Formerly, in my attempts to isolate the talent, I deducted, so to speak, from what I heard the part itself, a part common to all the actresses who appeared as *Phèdre*, which I had myself studied beforehand so that I might be capable of subtracting it, of receiving in the strained residue only the talent of Mme. Berma. But this talent which I sought to discover outside the part itself was indissolubly one with it. So with a great musician . . . his playing is become so transparent, so full of what he is interpreting, that himself one no longer sees and he is nothing now but a window opening upon a great work of art (I, 747).

So this is a sort of triumph, but one which we ought not to overestimate—it occurs in "this hour of indifference"—or accept as a final resolution to our question. In fact Marcel tells us a page later that "My own impression . . . though more pleasant than on the earlier occasion, was not really different. Only, I no longer put it to the test of a preexistent, abstract and false idea of dramatic genius, and I understood now that dramatic genius was precisely this" (I, 748).

This stage of the way is summarized on the next page in a beautiful and bitter aphorism: "We feel in one world, we think, we give names to things in another; between the two we can establish a certain correspondence, but not bridge the interval."

And another: "the difference that there is between a person, or a work of art which is markedly individual and the idea of beauty, exists just as much between what they make us feel and the idea of love, or of admiration. Wherefore we fail to recognise them" (I, 749).

As for that tertium quid, the way of bridging the interval, that is the substance of the book, of the whole book. We know it already, in a sense, for it was present in the madeleine, in the trees of Martinville, and elsewhere. It is in those moments, always mysterious in their compound of accident, independence, and fatefulness, moments such as another poet also has spoken of:

> To be conscious is not to be in time
> But only in time can the moment in the rose garden,
> The moment in the arbour where the rain beat,
> The moment in the draughty church at smokefall
> Be remembered; involved with past and future.
> Only through time time is conquered.*

And Marcel, as far as we have got with him, is in the position described by that poet in another place: We had the experience, but we missed the meaning.

*T. S. Eliot, "Burnt Norton."

XII

"Combray"—Topics. In General.

1. The novel as "private interpretation," as therefore "subversive." Compare the Reformation and the vernacular Bible.

2. The novel and the drama compared. Prose and poetry as means.

3. Objectivity of the drama; and its allegorical action demanding broad treatment.

4. Development of the novel away from fable, fabliau, romance, nouvelle; development of analysis, concern with "states of the soul," interior experience. Note by the way that poetry in the nineteenth century feels the pull, the temptation, to inwardness: Wordsworth, "Prelude," monologues of Browning, a fantasy of Shelley such as "The Witch of Atlas." Generally, though, the hypnotic regularity of poetry tends to work against the detailed exploration of idiosyncratic states of mind and private situations. So also does its commitment to ritual and magical origins.

5. Drama as communally, novel as privately, received.

6. On the treatment of interior experience, compare a soliloquy of Hamlet, *e.g.*, act 4, sc. 4, li. 32ff., with a soliloquy of Fabrice (*Charterhouse*, Anchor edn., 171–72). Limits of this comparison: not that one is "dramatic" and the other not; both are relevant, but the novelist's idea of relevance is much broader and at the same time less general than that of the playwright; if you compare, also,

the view of character taken in Greek drama, you see that the idea of relevance there is stricter still, for character in antiquity is situation and nothing more—about Oedipus we learn nothing irrelevant to the single action.

7. Dissolving of the limits of objectivity and situation in the novel. In, for example, Jane Austen we are left in no doubt that a situation exists. Characters may be mistaken about it, but the situation exists independently of their views. From Stendhal, perhaps, this solidity breaks up, and we see (a) attention focused on the character's receipt of experience as much as on the experience itself, and (b) the novelist's technical and artistic attention focused upon the way in which experience is received and interpreted, more than upon an "objective" action. So for Flaubert and James the style becomes the subject, and no subject exists independently of its artistic treatment. So also, instead of heroic actions on the world's stage we have the contemplation of private lives. Stendhal again is the balancing point, coupling heroic actions with ironic speculations on the possibility of heroic action in the nineteenth century. Compare I, 15, on recognition:

> Even the simple act which we describe as "seeing some one we know" is, to some extent, an intellectual process. We pack the physical outline of the creature we see with all the ideas we have already formed about him, and in the complete picture of him which we compose in our minds those ideas have certainly the principal place. In the end they come to fill out so completely the curve of his cheeks, to follow so exactly the line of his nose, they blend so harmoniously in the sound of his voice that these seem to be no more than a transparent envelope, so that each time we see the face or hear the voice it is our own ideas of him which we recognise and to which we listen.

8. Compare *The Magic Mountain* and *Ulysses* and *Remembrance of Things Past* with respect to subject and technique.

9. See I, 64, on the novel and character:

> These were the events which took place in the book I was reading. It is true that the people concerned in them were not what Françoise would have called "real people." But none of the feelings which the joys or misfortunes of a "real" person awaken in us can be awakened except through a mental picture of those joys or misfortunes; and the ingenuity of the first novelist lay in his understanding that, as the picture was the one essential element in the complicated structure of our emotions, so that simplification of it which

consisted in the suppression, pure and simple, of "real" people would be a decided improvement. A "real" person, profoundly as we may sympathise with him, is in a great measure perceptible only through our senses, that is to say, he remains opaque, offers a dead weight which our sensibilities have not the strength to lift. If some misfortune comes to him, it is only in one small section of the complete idea we have of him that we are capable of feeling any emotion; indeed it is only in one small section of the complete idea he has of himself that he is capable of feeling any emotion either. The novelist's happy discovery was to think of substituting for those opaque sections, impenetrable by the human spirit, their equivalent in immaterial sections, things, that is, which the spirit can assimilate to itself. After which it matters not that the actions, the feelings of this new order of creatures appear to us in the guise of truth, since we have made them our own, since it is in ourselves that they are happening, that they are holding in thrall, while we turn over, feverishly, the pages of the book, our quickened breath and staring eyes.

In one of the earliest of this series of lectures I compared Proust's novel with Dante's *Comedy*, briefly indicating by the literal comparison of their beginnings how both works were about *awakening*, and showing that for Proust as for Dante this awakening has a symbolic and even a religious sense: it means awakening from the sleep of sin, of the slothfulness Proust calls habit, or custom; and this awakening initiates a process in which the narrator plumbs the mysteries of iniquity and death as a means to purging himself and being born again as another, a poet, whose discovery of his vocation, or salvation, will enable him to begin the work of art which his readers are just finishing.

Now some work done by a friend seems to make possible a more detailed specifying of such a comparison. For I have just come upon an essay by Kenneth Burke, called "Catharsis: Second View,"* which I must have missed when it first appeared in 1959, in which, with the *Purgatorio* as model, he seeks to itemize the "requirements" for catharsis, that is, the general laws governing all stories about cleansing and regeneration. He finds thirteen such specifications. I shan't read you the whole list at once, because you'd only

*In Sheldon Norman Grebstein (ed.), *Perspectives in Contemporary Criticism* (New York, 1968), 277–78.

forget it, but take up each point serially, commenting on the comparisons as we go along.

I should preface my demonstration by saying that its working should be of interest not only in respect to Proust's book, but also with respect to the general question of what literary criticism is and does, or tries to do; to the extent that it works it will be a test of Burke's analytic prowess as well as of my ability at finding parallels; and it will be an illustration in action of that sort of criticism, sometimes called "archetypal," which seeks the simplest and most general laws governing works of similar kind; laws, indeed, like those which Proust himself, increasingly as he advances in his novel, claims to be its goal.

Burke: "Thus, tentatively making an 'existentialist' recipe for catharsis as contrived in Dante's *Purgatorio*, we might list 'requirements' of this sort:

> 1. "The purgand, to be purged, must contemplate, as an engaged observer, the sufferings, regrets, and efforts of other people."

This requires almost no comment, for it is evident that Marcel does so; in effect, "engaged observer" is an accurate description of his participation, as he observes others attempting to scale the heights of social "blessedness" even while he himself is making the same attempt.

> 2. "He must proceed by orderly stages through the realms of the damned, the penitent, and the blessed, with each such stage divided into rationally distinguishable substages."

On this point, I'd remind you of Professor Hindus' suggestive simile: it is as if, he said, Proust is trying to write the *Divine Comedy* without Christianity. This will obviously make for differences. If Dante's blessed are "the elect," Proust's blessed are "the elite." With the addition that the elite are also for Proust the irrevocably damned. It is obvious enough that Marcel has experience of the damned, the penitent, and the blessed; to what extent may we say that he proceeds through their realms by orderly stages?

Now Dante's order is arithmetical and spatial; though he takes a journey in time, all that he witnesses is in eternity. All the articulations of human behavior, with examples of each, are spread out in 3 canticles of 33 cantos apiece, prefaced by a prologue that perfects the number of the whole at 100. Within each canticle there are certain main divisions—for instance, the *Inferno* divides first into Incontinence, Violence, and Fraud—and further subdivided so as to make up into 10 categories—in the *Inferno,* 9 circles plus the ante-Inferno of the Trimmers.

But Proust's, or Marcel's, journey does not take him through eternity except in the special sense that any writer exhibiting a very large range of human figures invites comparison with the sculptures of Los's Halls (which tell every story possible to be experienced), it takes him through time, and this in a number of ways which nonetheless may be seen as "by orderly stages."

A. The story is told as from both ends of life at once, alternatively by Marcel the little boy and by Marcel the old man at Tansonville dreaming of what is past. And we see the little boy become, in orderly enough fashion, first an adolescent, then a young man, then a somewhat older young man, until he phases as it were invisibly into the old man who has been there from the very first paragraph.

B. Marcel's experience is represented also as expanding by orderly stages from his bedroom at Combray to Combray itself, to Balbec, to Paris; and these expansions are to some extent correlated with his progression up the social hierarchy, which is comically viewed as a progression toward (social) salvation, acceptance among the elite. From his middle-class family in rustic Combray he ascends from one drawing room to a better to the very best: from Mme. de Villeparisis' to the Duc de Guermantes' to a party at the Prince de Guermantes'. On the way he observes the progress of other earnest climbers after this kind of salvation: Bloch, Legrandin, Mme. Verdurin, Odette . . . and of others far more highly placed but now going down: Swann, Charlus.

C. The simplicity of this design is complicated, however, by this circumstance: the social hierarchy, which corresponds to Dante's hierarchy, is not eternal, and in fact is represented as a process of growth matched by corruption, as a stable form composed of ever-changing and replacing particles, as in the image of the fountain of Hubert Robert at II, 43 (see above, p. 115). One agency of this change is money, but another perhaps more central is vice, especially homosexuality. This introduces an ambiguous factor into social relations, that is, in being introduced to M. de Charlus, is Marcel going "up" or "down"? The obvious answer is up, but inasmuch as the Baron is going down already, from frequenting his kinfolk the Guermantes to the Verdurin salon, to rejection by the Verdurins, to male brothels, the police court, etc., the obvious answer is oddly shadowed

D. There are other complications as well. It is obvious that salvation through society is a mockery; it is in fact damnation: the climb proves to be a descent and a degradation. But there are other possibilities of salvation: friendship, love, art. Friendship need not be much discussed, for Marcel in several places dismisses it brusquely as an ideal. Love and art will be more appropriately discussed under other of Burke's "requirements" for purgation. To the present point I need say only that there are respects in which Marcel's progress in love and art may be thought of as orderly: to each stage in his conquest of society belongs a new love affair, though the woman does not always correspond to the social advance; so he goes from Gilberte to Odette to Oriane to Albertine. Similarly, though one could not say he "progresses" toward art at all, if that word mean steady advance by orderly stages, yet his life comes under the aegis successively of several artists or their arts: Bergotte, Berma, Elstir, the septuor of Vinteuil. The art which is his vocation, however, and true salvation and the real subject of his book, comes not by stages but by instantaneous revelations—revelations which by themselves tell little or nothing but require to be completed by hard work and thought and recollection. The two halves of the Proustian experience—the momentary vision and the long labor of writing—correspond nicely with Dante's report of his vision of the godhead,

> Un punto solo m'e maggior letargo
>   che venticinque secoli alla impresa
>   che fe' Nettuno ammirar l'ombra d'Argo.
>
> One moment alone was to me a greater oblivion [or
>   exhaustion; *letargo* combines the two]

> than five-and-twenty centuries were to the enterprise
> that made Neptune marvel at the shadow of the Argo.

where we see the one instantaneous and blinding moment equated
with exactly its opposite, the long fatigue of human history.

> 3. "He must have a male guide (a 'father') whom he greatly
> admires, but behind this guide there must be a Madonna-
> like woman whom he had revered on earth, and whom he
> will see when he has been properly prepared."

The artists I have just named do not serve Marcel as Virgil did
Dante. Though the painter Elstir in a marvelous eloquent passage
(I, 649) expresses the purgatorial aspect of the artist's progress
toward wisdom—"a journey through the wilderness which no one
else can take for us, an effort which no one can spare us . . . our
wisdom is the point of view from which we come at last to regard
the world"—and though Vinteuil's music becomes mysteriously
exemplary for Marcel of the ideal of art, Bergotte's encourage-
ments, on the other hand, return to him as bitter mockery in the
time of abysmal despair that preludes his self-discovery (II, 991).
Nevertheless the correspondence does exist: Marcel's guide is
Swann, and Swann leads to woman—through Odette to woman in
general or deified as Astarte, Aphrodite, Venus—but also to a
Madonna-like woman indeed, Marcel's mother.

Swann, of course, is only secondarily guide and lecturer like
Virgil. His first function is to guide Marcel by being his model, the
life he will imitate and surpass. I remarked in one of the earliest
lectures with what Freudian piety, in independence of Freud,
Proust begins his novel by dramatizing the Oedipal situation, and
how Swann so replaces the father as the dominant figure in Marcel's
life that the father is scarce heard of again after that first episode,
while what Burke would call the "representative anecdote" of
Swann's affair with Odette is told in considerable detail and plainly
regarded as somehow determinative of Marcel's affair with Albertine.

I may add that the correspondence is piquantly particular in
other ways. As Dante the Christian surpasses—in experience and
in his poem—Virgil the pagan, so Marcel the artist surpasses Swann
the connoisseur. It is tempting to add that Marcel the Christian

surpasses Swann the Jew, but I cannot quite remember Marcel's religion ever being explicitly mentioned, even if it is clear from, for example, what is said of Tante Léonie that the family is Catholic.

The nucleus of the entire novel is, we have seen, the episode of the good-night kiss. Swann, by coming to visit, threatens to deprive the child of his mother's kiss, thought of as a viaticum,* at bedtime. By an unexpected reversal, however, the real effect will be to secure the child his mother's presence through the entire night, with consequences he will then and later view as both good and bad, but which at any rate resound throughout the novel.

The good-night kiss is viewed by Marcel as the model for his relations with Albertine when, like his mother, she lives in his house and may or may not be accessible:

> It was no longer the peace of my mother's kiss at Combray that I felt when I was with Albertine on these evenings, but, on the contrary, the anguish of those on which my mother scarcely bade me good night, or even did not come up at all to my room, whether because she was vexed with me or was kept downstairs by guests. This anguish—not merely its transposition in terms of love—no, this anguish itself which had at one time been specialised in love, which had been allocated to love alone when the division, the distribution of the passions took effect, seemed now to be extending again to them all, became indivisible again as in my childhood, as though all my sentiments which trembled at the thought of my not being able to keep Albertine by my bedside, at once as a mistress, a sister, a daughter; as a mother too of whose regular good-night kiss I was beginning again to feel the childish need, had begun to coalesce, to unify in the premature evening of my life which seemed fated to be as short as a day in winter. But if I felt the anguish of my childhood, the change of person that made me feel it, the difference of the sentiment that it inspired in me, the very transformation in my character, made it impossible for me to demand the soothing of that anguish from Albertine as in the old days from my mother (II, 456).

At the very end, after relentlessly driving home in numerous variations the point that art comes not from intellect and culture but only from suffering, and that suffering comes only from woman— any woman, so long as after attracting us she fails one night to put herself at our disposal—he returns to the episode of the good-night

*This word *viaticum*, used of Albertine's kiss also, occurs once more in a funny way. A kinsman of the Guermantes is dying and is said to have already received the viaticum. His nickname is Mama.

kiss once again, and here it is regarded, in a passage that brings together ever so many strands of the narrative, as the first cause of Marcel's life altogether:

It was that evening, when my mother abdicated her authority, which marked the commencement of the waning of my will power and my health, as well as the beginning of my grandmother's lingering death. Everything was predetermined from the moment when, unable any longer to endure the idea of waiting until the morning to press a kiss upon my mother's face, I made up my mind, jumped out of bed and, in my nightshirt, went and sat by the window through which the moonlight came, until I heard M. Swann leave. My parents had accompanied him to the door; I heard the door open, the bell tinkle and the door shut again. Even at this moment, in the mansion of the Prince de Guermantes, I heard the sound of my parents' footsteps as they accompanied M. Swann and the reverberating, ferruginous, interminable, sharp, jangling tinkle of the little bell which announced to me that at last M. Swann had gone and Mamma was going to come upstairs—I heard these sounds again, the very identical sounds themselves, although situated so far back in the past (II, 1122).

So the equation: Swann leads to the mother as Virgil leads to Beatrice, is specifiable. Marcel does not, it is true, literally meet up with his mother as Dante does with Beatrice; but she is revealed to him as the spiritual form that has determined the course of his life.

    4. "All stages of the purgation proper must be under the sign of blessing (as with the singing of a Beatitude in each circle of the Purificatory Mount, while he proceeds towards the Woman Who Blesses)."

This point doesn't seem to suggest any exact fit at all. But I remind myself that Burke is discussing not the whole *Comedy* but especially the *Purgatorio*. And I might hazard this: for Proust, paradise or blessedness comes uniquely in the form of those experiences represented first by the madeleine and last by the things that happen at the beginning of the last episode, where several of them occur in quick succession. Now the rest of that last episode, the grotesque masquerade ball put on by Time, together with Marcel's reflections on his vocation, does indeed represent his Purgatory: he repents of his life and of his former indifference; because he is now "pregnant" with a book he thinks with apprehension about death and illness, regrets the time he has wasted, and sees himself as ready, if granted time, to amend. These reflections return over and over during the chapter, but it seems fair to say that, as they have been set off by his discovery of a vocation in art (which began the chapter) they do come "under the sign of blessing."

> 5. "The purgand's guide must generously keep him reminded that later there will be a change to a guide more highly qualified (an important point, because this arrangement in effect allows for a 'transference' of allegiance without the need of 'father-rejection')."

Again, not literally true. Swann doesn't *remind* Marcel of anything. But if you grant that Virgil *guides* Dante's steps while Swann serves as *model* for Marcel's, the correspondence is clear. The critical event of Swann's life is the suffering caused by a woman, and so it will be for Marcel, with the difference that for Marcel this suffering will be understood as necessary to its own transcendence in art, as necessary to purgation.

> 6. "About midway in his development, spurred by study precisely at a time when most threatened by sloth, the purgand must have all motivation authoritatively reduced for him to terms of a single impulse ('love') with its corresponding problems and hierarchy."

It is in Canto XVII of the *Purgatorio*, as near as not to the middle point of the *Comedy*, that Virgil explains to Dante in what way the life of the world is based on love perverted, defective, excessive. They are at that time in the circle of the slothful.

That sloth, accidia, what Chaucer finds the wonderful word *wanhope* for, is Marcel's besetting sin needs no arguing. Of ever so many places where he describes this condition one might best remember the passage where he continually resolves to become a writer "tomorrow" and wonders why tomorrow never comes, finding the answer that the purity and wholesomeness of "tomorrow," when all things will be possible, become corrupt from one only circumstance, his own arrival therein.

Anyhow, as near as not to the middle point of his novel—in the English edition it occurs at the beginning of the second of the two volumes, with roughly eleven hundred pages to either side of it—Marcel has all motivation authoritatively reduced for him to terms of a single impulse, love, though in the "diabolically" parodied form of homosexual love. After being, as we saw earlier, in rather comical doubts about the precise nature of the oddities he has observed in M. de Charlus' behavior, it is revealed to him that the Baron is a homosexual. This discovery sets off an extraordinary meditation indeed—sermon, diatribe, clinical description, epical and prophetic passion, all are involved.

The entire episode is in the form of an extended comparison. The Duchesse has in her courtyard a plant which can be fertilized only by a particular species of insect, and Marcel is watching this plant, "exposed in the courtyard with that insistence with which mothers 'bring out' their marriageable offspring," and wondering idly enough whether the "unlikely insect" will arrive that very morning, when he sees Charlus' meeting with Jupien and so stations himself as to hear its sequel. This comparison between one unlikely relation and another, begins the episode, ends the episode, and is invoked in various ways throughout it. For example,

> M. de Charlus had distracted me from looking to see whether the bee was bringing to the orchid the pollen it had so long been waiting to receive, and had no chance of receiving save by an accident so unlikely it might be called a sort of miracle. But this was a miracle also that I had just witnessed, almost of the same order and no less marvellous. As soon as I had considered their meeting from this point of view, everything about it seemed to me instinct with beauty. The most extraordinary devices that nature has invented to compel insects to ensure the fertilisation of flowers which without their intervention could not be fertilised because the male flower is too far away from the female—or when, if it is the wind that must provide for the transportation of the pollen, she makes that pollen so much more simply detachable from the male, so much more easily arrested in its flight by the female flower, by eliminating the secretion of nectar which is no longer of any use since there is no insect to be attracted, and, that the flower may be kept free for the pollen which it needs, which can fructify only in itself, makes it secrete a liquid which renders it immune to all other pollens—seemed to me no more marvellous than the existence of the subvariety of inverts destined to guarantee the pleasures of love to the invert who is growing old: men who are attracted not by all other men, but—by a phenomenon of correspondence and harmony similar to those that precede the fertilisation of heterostyle trimorphous flowers like the *lythrum salicoria*—only by men considerably older than themselves (II, 22–23).

Now Burke's "requirement" speaks of *all* motivation, and this scene might seem not to meet the demand in *all*, for even in the same passage it is amply admitted that there are men who really do love women and are not homosexual. And yet the universal nature of the homosexual's affliction—when Marcel uses the term *vice* he assures us: "we use the word for convenience only"—is amply attested: it is love, it exists everywhere, it corrupts everything. "These descendants of the Sodomites, so numerous that we may apply to them that other verse of Genesis: 'if a man can number the dust of the earth, then shall thy seed also be numbered'."—which is the Lord's word to Abraham about the establishment of the Chosen People—"have established themselves throughout the entire world." They are compared over and over to the Jews: it would be a mistake, says Marcel, to start a Sodomist movement on the lines of the Zionist movement, with the object of rebuilding Sodom, for the Sodomites would not live there but would spread again throughout the world: "in other words, everything would go on very much as it does today in London, Berlin, Rome, Petrograd or Paris."

One can see by the tone of this long-sustained harangue, rather violently different from anything else in Proust—indignation, justice, sympathy, and perhaps fear are struggling in it, and among the worst things about homosexuals is the sin against the mother: "sons without a mother, to whom they are obliged to lie all her life long and even in the hour when they close her dying eyes"—that something of extreme importance, not altogether contained in the fictive terms of the novel, obtrudes itself here; and the discoveries of biographers will reveal to us what it is and to a certain extent why it is so. But that is outside the present realm of relevance, and I may conclude by reiterating the gist of Burke's terms for this requirement: Marcel has all motivation authoritatively reduced for him to terms of a single impulse, love; what moves the sun and the other stars, and what brings the bee to the orchid, and what brings Jupien to fertilize—"the word fertilise must be understood in a moral sense," says our author—M. de Charlus.

7. "He must accept a distinction in kind between a 'natural' and a 'spiritual' or 'rational' order of motives. And maybe

we should treat as cathartically essential the etymologically accidental fact that the root of the word for the 'higher' kind of motive (*d'animo—Purgatorio* xvii, 93) also provides a generic term for the lower kind: 'animal'."

This requirement is a hard one to meet because in the first place I'm not sure I understand it. Reference to the place cited reveals the context: Virgil is telling Dante that neither the Creator nor any creature was ever without love, and that this love may be either natural or *d'animo*, for which my translation gives "rational" but which I should rather read as something like "belonging to the will." Natural love, in medieval terms, would be exemplified by the force of gravity explainable as the stone's will to fall to a lower place; and the same term, *gravezza*, serves for the sins that cause people to fall into hell.

But taking into account a line of speculation Burke has pursued in many places besides the essay I am basing upon at present, that every spiritual thing having to do with purgation will be accompanied by its bodily parody, I find I am able to offer a suggestion after all. It has to do with bathrooms.

Our natural necessities, which ought to make democrats of us all, turn up in Proust's novel as a mockery of social hierarchy and its invidiousness. The point is driven home chiefly by the remark of Marcel's grandmother about the marquise who keeps the public conveniences in the Champs-Elysées (those cubicles where men crouch like sphinxes, says Marcel at an earlier mention of these) and who has been giving a harangue on the social discrimination with which she runs her business: "Could anything have been more typical of the Guermantes, or the Verdurins and their little circle? Heavens, what fine language she put it all in" (I, 938). But other references to excrement seem typically to appear in relation to society and social distinctions, as for instance when Oriane and Swann joke a bit crudely about Mme. de Cambremer's name and its likeness to *le mot de Cambronne*; or even more crudely when M. de Charlus, in the height of his insolence and pride, says: "As for all the little people who call themselves Marquis de Cambremerde or de Vatefairefiche . . . It doesn't matter whether you go and p——s at Comtesse S——t's or s——t at Baronne P——s's, it's exactly the same, you will have compromised yourself and have used a dirty rag instead of toilet paper. Which is not nice" (II, 348).*

There are probably not enough references of this sort to make the relation entirely clear. But recalling that the underground stalls in the Champs-Elysées relate to disease by the fact that it is there that Marcel's grandmother has her first stroke, we may add the butler's anecdote about M. de Charlus, identifiable by his yellow trousers, standing so long in the *pissotière:* he must, says the butler, have caught a disease. "That's what comes of running after the girls at his age" (II, 511). And right at the beginning of the novel (I, 10) Marcel identifies the bathroom of his childhood home as a sacred place, a "place of refuge," "the only room whose door I was allowed to lock," belonging to "inviolable solitude" and to reading, dreaming, weeping, as well as "a more special and baser use."

So natural functions seem to relate on one hand to social distinctions and disease, on the other to the sufferings of love and art, a fair enough reflection of the division of the entire novel in its exterior and interior aspects.

The evidence is not massive by any means. But such as it is, it is reasonably unequivocal in offering, or playing upon, a distinction in kind between natural and spiritual or rational motives. Perhaps it would have been safer to begin with to satisfy this requirement by speaking of social climbing as "natural" and the life of art as "spiritual." But we got there, or somewhere near it, all the same, by underground.

    8. "He must have so strong a sense of wonder that references to wonder recur like an *idée fixe* throughout the text."

I think this needs little or no demonstration, whether we think of the young Marcel's comically naive astonishment at the discovery of one after another social obliquity or of the *moments bienséants,* or the sufferings of love that interrupt the trivial dullness of quotidian custom.

    9. "He must have confronted a basic conflict of authorities (spiritual and temporal), where the spiritual authorities are

---

*The elided words in the translation are, in the original, *pipi* and *caca,* with no letters omitted.

in a state of corruption that he looks upon as infecting the temporal."

For Dante this will have been the conflict of empire and papacy chiefly, with Boniface the Eighth as a prominent example of the corruption of spiritual authority. For Proust it is rather less clear, though it seems true in a very general way. Some more particular notions may be advanced, though: the true nobility of society is enshrined in the Guermantes spirit, particularly in Oriane, and the exterior progression of the novel represents the corruption of this spirit, identified with mythology and medieval France, until the person embodying the name of Princesse de Guermantes, at the end, is actually Mme. Verdurin. In an oblique way the substantial though intermittent consideration given to the Dreyfus case is also a confronting of basic conflict. And, third, there is Marcel's own life, which for all but the last hundred and fifty pages of the novel is in a condition of such conflict, with the spiritual authority decisively represented by art corrupt in him and infecting the temporal with boredom, illness, fatigue, apathy, and the feeling that nothing is worth doing.

10. "At stages along the way, the purgand must have dreams that foreshadow the course of his development."

Literal dreams, no, or at least only a few, and those few not especially decisive. If we are permitted to include daydream and fantasy and meditation, however, Marcel meets the specification many times over (a good many more than Dante, for that matter).

11. "He must accept it without question that people are cleansed by willingly undergoing hardships to make amends for previous laxities."

This is of course the burden of the narrator's last meditations, as it had been of Elstir's sermon on wisdom, as it had been of the famous reflection upon Vermeer at the time of Bergotte's death. Dozens of places might be cited, I choose one of the best-known: "instinct dictates the duty to be done and intelligence supplies the excuses for evading it. But in art excuses count for nothing; good intentions are of no avail; the artist must at every instant heed his instinct; so that art is the most real of all things, the sternest school in life and truly the Last Judgment" (II, 1001).

12. "He must forever be pressing onwards and upwards, despite occasional lapses."

One might rephrase this a bit for Marcel; forever lapsing, he does get onwards and upwards in the end. And since the interior progression of the book is the discovery of an artistic vocation, which is held to be the same as salvation, the formula fits fairly enough.

13. "At every stage, there must be a language of imagery corresponding to a language of ideas—and these ideas must have their explicit expression, too, not being merely suggested through their imagistic counterparts."

Burke doesn't expand on this rather cryptic "requirement" with reference to Dante. At the simplest, the imagery referred to will mean the description of the sinners and their punishments, which are appropriate—as the lustful burn in refining fires, and so on—while the language of ideas will mean the *theory* according to which the sinners become exemplary illustrations; the theory shows what they are examples *of*, perverse, defective, excessive love, as described by Virgil at the middle point of the *Purgatorio*. Among Dante's own ten requirements for his poem in the letter to Can Grande, the last one is *exemplorum positivus*; the translation I remember gives "proceeding by means of examples," but I suggest "affirmed by examples" or "driven home by examples" as possibly more illuminating.

But when I turn from Dante, and just look at Burke's sentence, it seems to make a natural fit with what happens in Proust; indeed, as I was never quite happy with the term *image clusters*, I propose to adapt Burke's phrase and speak to you now of Proust's *language of imagery* in adverting once more—for the last time—to a characteristic of his composition I barely described in an earlier lecture. Here, too, I hope you will understand sympathetically, I must make an exception to my usual practice because of the nature of the subject, and quote very extensively a number of examples.

My first example, in that early lecture, was Proust's very first paragraph, and what I found there I was able to back up with the inspection of several other paragraphs in the first few pages; so that the constancy of what looked like a quite complex set of associated relations suggested we did indeed have something like a key to the author's mode of imagination, though I was uncertain—and am so still—whether it will unlock any door that leads anywhere. Nevertheless, I made a fairly large claim, or two claims: in many paragraphs, I said, the same atoms, so to say, go to form very different structures, in which the formal relationships are constant while material, particulars, tone, vary considerably; and I suggested that this way of composing might have something to say about the entire work. And I made an abstract of ten elements, most of all of which are very often found together. I remind you of them in the order in which they came up in my first couple of examples.

(1) a uniquely Proustian attention to *ambience,* qualities of air, light, darkness, color—a species of impressionist rendering in words—led on to (2) reference to a work of art, which involved allusion to (3) religious or mythological figures or stories as well as (4) history. There then would follow two categories closely linked as the obverse and reverse of the same (5) disguise or transformation of the thing or things seen and (6) specification of some peculiarity or distortion in the way of seeing. All this would be accompanied by (7) a reference to travel, most often by train, a reference to nature, most often a flower, and (8) a curiously particular category involving the mention of some mechanical instrument, most often optical (9) but in any case almost always having to do with a mechanical means of affecting perception. Finally, there would be a pointed allusion to (10) a name, and some striking circumstance having to do with names and naming.

Though these categories ought in several instances to overlap—as a reference to art, mythology, religion, or history, is almost bound to involve the mention of a proper name—it is remarkable that in ever so many instances we can fill up the form without using one particular twice. Thus on pages 7 and 8 of Volume I we have several names—Combray, Golo, Geneviève de Brabant, which refer us to history and myth or legend; but the category of *name* is filled by a special attention to "the old gold sonorous name of Brabant" in a separate reference.

The next step, before trying to decide what if anything all this means, is to check out a few of the very many places at which it seems to happen that Proust writes in this language of imagery. And one of the first things I see is that this language is not available only for set descriptive pieces, but may come up in the very moment of such action as this novel goes in for; a first example (I, 179) is Swann's kissing Odette. (See, also, above, p. 52):

1. Air, light, etc. "she fixed her eyes on him with that languishing and solemn air . . . her brilliant eyes . . . like two great tears."

2. Art. "the old Florentine's paintings." Swann has already seen Odette as Zipporah in a Botticelli painting.

3. Religion, myth. "pagan scenes as well as scriptural."

4. History. Not here literally, though a moment later their phrase for making love "served to commemorate in their vocabulary the long forgotten custom from which it sprang."

5. Disguise. "her attitude was . . . one which she knew was appropriate to such moments, and was careful not to forget to assume."

6. Way of seeing. Swann sees her as in an old Florentine painting, and he also fixes on her features, delaying the kiss, on the features of an Odette not yet kissed, "that comprehensive gaze" with which a traveler tries to memorize the view of a country to which he may never return.

7. Travel. The traveler just mentioned. But we need not overlap; they are in fact traveling in a carriage at the time of the kiss.

8. Nature, most often a flower. Odette's flowers are his pretext for kissing her.

9. Optical or other instrument. Not here.

10. Name. The flowers were a kind of orchid named cattleya, and this name is particularly remarked as becoming their metaphor, "a simple verb which they would employ without a thought of its original meaning."

In this passage we score eight out of ten, or possibly a skimpy nine.

I. 37. In the initial description of Combray we have (1) the shadows of the gables, the colors, the smell of cooking, (2) primitive painting, (3) the solemn names of saints, (4) medieval ramparts of the town, (5) so remote a corner of my memory, painted in colors so different from those in which the world is decked for me today, (6) the streets seem to me . . . insubstantial, (7) as we used to see it from the railway, (8) the houses compared with sheep, (9) the magic lantern, (10) Golo, Geneviève, Combray, various names of saints, of streets.

I, 293. In the initial description of the room at Balbec: (1) a finer air, azure-tinted, saline, (2) interior decoration, (3) Legrandin on the fishermen, the description of the Church with Apostles and Virgin, (4) Middle Ages, (5) the sea reflected from the bookcases, (6) longing to see an ocean storm, less as a mighty spectacle than as a momentary revelation of the true life of nature, (7) the good, the generous train at one twenty-two, (8) frail but hardy plants, (9) phonograph, mechanical imitations of a storm, illuminated fountains, "the mechanical inventions of mankind," (10) the name Balbec and its difference from the reality, the stations of the train "magnificently surcharged with names."

From this example I note a tendency of such language to extend itself so that the various images repeat themselves in numerous examples over a long passage, in this instance I, 293–301. The whole passage comes under the title "Place Names: The Name," so it is successively the names of, for example, Florence, Parma, the stations of the train, Venice, that set off items in the other categories, as, *e.g.*, Balbec is associated with magnifying glasses, Venice with a photograph, Parma with the reproduction of paintings, and so on.

Here are a few other examples in which a great many though possibly not all the categories are represented:

> I, 566–67, preluding the introduction of Charlus.
> I, 720–21, the name of Guermantes.
> I, 1016–17, meditation of the past.
> I, 1017–18, Elstir's paintings.
> I, 1023, Parma (compare 296).
> I, 1031, racial qualities of the Guermantes.

I might leave it at that, saying no more than: this is the way in which the world occurs to this great artist, as the richest sort of complex of sense-impressions, reading, revery, still consonant with a certain definiteness of structure; adding perhaps a not-very-precise idea I have that the resort to this language of imagery much diminishes during the second half of the novel. Much diminishes—or else the elements get spread over longer passages than even a long paragraph or two or three. The latter seems to happen, for one instance, in the revelation of M. de Charlus' true nature that takes up a couple of dozen pages at the beginning of "Cities of the Plain." I think it fair to say that all the items I have taken to exemplify our ten categories turn up, many of them more than once, but not in so close a conjunction as before. For example:

On page 10 Charlus is speaking about how he tries to pick up young men, and in a few lines we have (7) a railroad journey, (4) an historic edifice which is (3) a cathedral, (10) names and naming: speaking in the feminine gender as we say "Is His Highness enjoying *her* usual health," (9) the lens of an optical penholder, and perhaps one or two more; but we never get the whole sequence together.

Now all this may be accidental, or at most circumstantial. Persons better qualified in French than I am have noticed that the character of the writing changes from—very roughly—the first half of the book to the second. Howard Moss notes about *Swann's Way* and *Within a Budding Grove* that "seen retrospectively, both volumes were written after disillusionment had set in. Yet both volumes create worlds more powerful than those that follow them. Proust is an extraordinary satirist and a superb thinker; but he is, when all is said and done, the great master of emanation . . . his boyhood and his adolescence provide material particularly suited to his supreme gifts. There is no world Proust cannot command; it is these two worlds, nevertheless, that are inimitable."* Whether we agree or no, *emanation* is a good word to discover and apply to these groups of images; emanation, evocation.

If we knew more about the history of the composition we might be able to offer another exterior reason for the change; the writer

*Moss, *Magic Lantern*, 82.

is old, tired, ill, he feels the near approach of death, there just isn't time to do everything in so expansive a manner as before, so genial a manner. And certain things said by Marcel toward the end of the work give color to this view.

Or else, looking about for a reason interior and intrinsic to the novel, it could be said that the style suitable for portraying relative innocence and closeness to nature in the first few volumes is not so appropriate to the devastations of the last few. But we remind ourselves that the language of imagery appears to turn up in social just as much as in natural descriptions.

So for a possible resolution to all this, I offer somewhat diffidently this hypothesis, which might work equally well if you thought the author had been conscious from the beginning of his odd method of constructing paragraphs or if you thought he became conscious of it at some point during the course of composition (that he could not have remained oblivious of it throughout is made clear, I think, from Albertine's parody of Marcel's manner (II, 468–699) (see above, p. 95).

Each element in the imagist language becomes dominant over a single part of the novel, and becomes subject to critical scrutiny; it becomes an equivalent language of ideas, in Burke's terms, and when it does this it may have the effect for the time of displacing the other elements, or at least of preventing their systematic and grouped appearance. I shall try to show very briefly how this might be so.

1. Ambience, atmosphere, what I spoke of as impressionism, seems dominant over all descriptions of places: Combray, Balbec, Venice, la Raspelière, as also over descriptions of Elstir's paintings and, less clearly, Vinteuil's music.

2. Art works rise into prominence at a number of places such as those just mentioned, coming to a climax in the narrator's meditations on his own projected work.

3. Religion or myth. As Fowlie has shown in an excellent essay, the Duchesse is always regarded as a mythological figure and

4. A person uniting myth and history. Brichot's etymologies might come in here under history too. But we shouldn't forget that

the novel which means also to be a memoir concerns itself with history directly: Dreyfus, the Great War.

5. Disguise or transformation of what is seen. The last chapter is a grotesque in which people are disguised indeed, by Time.

6. Peculiarity or distortion in the way of seeing. Thematic from the beginning. As (5) is what the book is about externally regarded—people do present false appearances, whether deliberately or not—then (6) is its equivalent internally regarded. One could go on about this for a long time, but by now I expect you see it plain enough.

7. Travel by train occupies the center of attention at a number of places, seconded by travel by carriage and by auto.

8. Nature, most often a flower. Swann's cattleyas, Mme. Swann portrayed as a kind of vegetation or hothouse goddess, the flower in the Duchesse's courtyard considered as an emblem for Charlus "fertilized" by Jupien.

9. The optical (or other sense-transforming) instrument. The magic lantern of the opening goes through many manifestations, not forgetting the telephone with its aura of communication from the dead, and emerges at the very end (II, 1113, 1118) as the novel itself: magnifying glass, optician of Combray . . . microscope, telescope:

> For, as I have already shewn, they would not be my readers but readers of themselves, my book serving merely as a sort of magnifying glass, such as the optician of Combray used to offer to a customer, so that through my book I would give them the means of reading in their own selves (II, 1113).

> Even those who were favourable to my conception of the truths which I intended later to carve within the temple congratulated me on having discovered them with a microscope when I had, on the contrary, used a telescope to perceive things which, it is true, were very small but situated afar off and each of them a world in itself (II, 1118).

10. Name. This is perhaps the most general title for the quest on which our hero goes: to see how things come into phase with their names; also how they don't. Maybe the quiet climax to this theme is the double recognition that Mme. Verdurin and Mlle. de Saint-Loup, the old bourgeoise harridan and Swann's granddaugh-

ter (and Odette's) have become Guermantes, so that in life as well as in geography, in time as in space, Swann's Way and the Guermantes Way turn out to be one.

finis

In Conclusion

The instructor who discourages his pupils from beginning the endings of their essays with "And so we see that . . . ," especially when no one has seen anything of the kind, or indeed anything much, had better forbid himself the same way out. But all the same there is something to be said, and he should try to say it.

"What has concluded, that we should conclude something about it?" was attributed by my teacher I. A. Richards to Benjamin Paul Blood, whom I have never seen quoted or cited by anyone else, ever. I did not conclude about Benjamin Paul Blood, however, that he never existed, only that after uttering his one luminous unilluminating sentence he retired to a hillside with other sages, I. A. Richards among them, and for all I know may be sitting there still. Looking unsuccessfully for that quotation, I was reading again in Richards' *Principles of Literary Criticism* and thought as I had a few times before that if the theory there advanced was not a good theory, nor likely to be furthered by whatever tremendous advances in the neural sciences, the book was nevertheless the book of a wise and gentle and good man; may something the same be worthily said of the rest of us.

I too had said, unconsciously following Benjamin Paul Blood, that teaching "was a process trying to look like a result." As a careful and consequential thinker, or teacher, I was only twelve years or so in producing the corollary: "yes, but isn't everything?" like history, I meant, and life and the world entire.

Freud had kindly enrolled teaching among his three impossible tasks: to rule, to heal, to teach. I continue to think it decent to be up there among the other impossibles. I got into the art, or trade, long before I had heard that or much of anything else, and also by accident and without advanced degrees. For in 1946, by the exemplary generosity of our government in establishing the G.I. Bill and so inducing colleges and universities to find warm bodies to put up against the veterans (twenty of them, and still in combat boots), I became a teacher, or anyhow a kind of dogsbody responsible for The Bible and Shakespeare and The Modern Novel and Modern Poetry (with my first book coming out, I was presumed to know something of that) and whatever else needed doing. It was the beginning of my education, and I remain grateful for it. Teacher and pupils were of an age, about twenty-six, and generally either friends or friendly, if only on the ground of deep and base suspicions of what we had got ourselves into.

This small book has been about teaching as well as about Proust, as any of you getting this far will have noticed. Many wonderful things have been said about teaching, and I will reproduce two while warning you that in spite of my admiration I can't afford either.

Plato comes first, as he should, and in the Seventh Letter (341 c–d) says of his own teaching, "There is no way of putting it in words like other studies. Acquaintance with it must come rather after a long period of instruction in the subject itself and of close companionship, when, suddenly, like a blaze kindled by a leaping spark, it is generated in the soul and at once becomes self-sustaining."

And Henry Adams, after two and a half millennia, adds: "Even to him education was a serious thing. A parent gives life, but as parent, gives no more. A murderer takes life, but his deed stops there. A teacher affects eternity; he can never tell where his influence stops."

How happy I am not to believe any of all that; but I think Adams more on the mark when he adds immediately after: "A teacher is expected to teach truth, and may perhaps flatter himself that he does so, if he stops with the alphabet and the multiplication table, as a mother teaches truth by making a child eat with a spoon; but morals are quite another truth and philosophy is more complex still." Teachers of Plato's kind may still exist. Some of Kenneth Burke's students at Bennington witness to the sort of illumination they experienced after months of bewilderment, when, about the end of April, the simplicity of Kenneth's teaching at last came through. And I once heard Stanley Edgar Hyman's last class in Myth & Ritual compared to "the reaping of the ear of corn, in silence, before the initiates at Eleusis"; though I think to remember it was Stanley himself who did the comparing, in a tone compounded inextricably of pride and self-mockery.

Altogether, though, it is a deficiency of teaching as an art form that it stops, without ending. And that it is all to do again. The common teacherly complaint that the students keep getting younger amply testifies to it. Mostly we teachers must finish, like surrogates for Henry Adams' mom, by reminding our pupils of the order of the alphabet and advising them to continue using a spoon on the soup. Philip Rieff's splendid book *Fellow Teachers* is a harangue so bracing—damn braces, says Blake, bless relaxes—that I read it every other year; but who could live up to it save its author alone? Our betters constantly admonished us, in our earlier years, that we must teach literature As Literature, not as an adjunct to history, psychology, philosophy, or (beneath all) the sociable sciences; but when I asked in meeting how I was supposed to do this, the subject changed.

There's a Buddhist anecdote I prefer even to Plato. A man in danger of being drowned in a flood grabbed hold of a raft that providentially came by, and was drifted to safety. In gratitude he strapped the raft to his back and carried it for the rest of his life. I couldn't have predicted the moral, Reader, and nor I think could you: So do all they that live by the doctrine.

But my favorite epitome of teaching and learning, one that works, I now see, in substance, form, and context, is one by Proust. It is remarkable how in old age, after following as best we could every fashion in history, psychology, aesthetics, and so on, we return to the moral; or maybe it isn't so remarkable, for M. H.

Abrams holds it is the most persistent and recurring idea of the function of letters in life from antiquity through the eighteenth century, and indeed it keeps showing through even the most sorbonnical refinements of the present moment.

The scene before us is this. Marcel, now adolescent, has made the acquaintance of the great painter Elstir, and is walking with him to Elstir's summer place at Balbec, when it suddenly occurs to him that this man of genius, this lonely sage and philosopher with his marvelous talk, master of all wisdom, may have been in his youth the silly and corrupt painter once taken up by the Verdurins and known as M. Biche. Marcel, remarkable as ever for his superb tact and social refinement, asks Elstir about this, and is answered. Elstir says that yes, he was indeed that man: "and as we were now already almost at his house, a man less distinguished of intelligence and spirit might perhaps have simply and a bit drily bade me farewell and afterward taken care never to see me again. But that was not how Elstir dealt with me." And now there enters another voice for a moment, that of the aged Marcel or that of Marcel Proust himself, another wise and deep master who had also been a silly and corrupt young man, and knew it: "In the style of a true master—and this was perhaps, from the point of view of pure artistry, the only way in which Elstir fell short of the true sense of mastery, for an artist, in order to live altogether in the truth of the life of the spirit, ought to be alone, and not spread himself around,* even among disciples—in every situation involving himself or others, he sought to draw out, for the better instruction of the young, the element of truth contained therein. So he now chose, in preference to words that might have avenged his pride, words that might teach me something." The brief sermon follows:

> "There is no one, however wise he may be," he said to me, "who has not at some time in his youth said things, or for that matter done things, which he hates to remember and would wish to have erased. But he ought not to regret them absolutely for he could not be certain of having become wise (in the degree to which that can happen at all), unless he had gone through all the foolish or hateful forms that had to lead up to that last of forms. I know that

*doit être seul, ok, but ne pas prodiguer de son moi—you can see why translators go mad.

there are young men, the sons and grandsons of remarkable men, whose tutors have instructed them since their schooldays in nobility of spirit and moral refinement. Perhaps they have nothing in their lives they need wish away, they might publish and sign everything they ever said, but they are pathetic persons, characterless children of pedants, whose wisdom is a nothingness and without issue. Wisdom is not had as a gift, one has to find it for oneself after a journey that no one can take for us nor spare us, for it is a point of view about experience. The lives you admire, the attitudes you find noble, were not arranged by parent or preceptor, they come from beginnings altogether different, being influenced by whatever fashion of wickedness or stupidity reigned around them. They stand for fight and victory. I can see that the portrait of what we were in early days is no longer recognizable to us, and would in any event be unpleasant to look at. But it ought not to be denied, for it is a witness that we have really lived, that out of the common elements of life, the life of the studio and artistic cliques (if we are talking about a painter), we have drawn something that goes beyond them." (P,I,863–64)

It was for the substance that I first admired and loved that passage, and still do. But as I copied it out I saw that in context it represented also the formal situation of teacher and pupil, for while Elstir has been talking Marcel has thought of little else but possibly seeing the little group of girls appear on his horizon, and of his disappointment at their failing to appear.

So there is teacher, handing out the platitudes—this is the order of the alphabet, eat your soup with a spoon—reveling in what a friend of my youth, now many years dead, called in his autobiography "the yes-they-are-Eternal Verities," while Marcel, or Lucretius' Memmius, or anyone in any class, is dreaming of love.

And so we see that.

hn, 5 viii 86